DEATH OF A DISCIPLINE

The Wellek Library Lectures in Critical Theory

The Wellek Library Lectures in Critical Theory are given annually at the University of California, Irvine, under the auspices of UCI Critical Theory. The following lectures were given in May 2000.

UCI Critical Theory
Gabriele Schwab, Director

PREVIOUSLY PUBLISHED WELLEK LIBRARY LECTURES

Postprint: Books and Becoming Computational (2021)
    N. Katherine Hayles

In the Ruins of Neoliberalism: The Rise of Antidemocratic Politics in the West (2019)
    Wendy Brown

Morphing Intelligence: From IQ Measurement to Artificial Brains (2019)
    Catherine Malabou

Knowledge, Power, and Academic Freedom (2019)
    Joan Wallach Scott

Dark Ecology: For a Logic of Future Coexistence (2016)
    Timothy Morton

Violence and Civility: On the Limits of Political Philosophy (2015)
    Étienne Balibar

Globalectics: Theory and the Politics of Knowing (2012)
    Ngugi wa Thiong'o

For a complete list of books in the series, please see the Columbia University Press website.

DEATH OF A DISCIPLINE

GAYATRI CHAKRAVORTY SPIVAK

TWENTIETH ANNIVERSARY EDITION

COLUMBIA UNIVERSITY PRESS   NEW YORK

Columbia University Press
Publishers Since 1893
New York Chichester, West Sussex
cup.columbia.edu
Preface to the Twentieth Anniversary Edition © 2023
Columbia University Press
Copyright © 2003 Columbia University Press
All rights reserved

Cataloging-in-Publication Data is available from the Library of Congress.

ISBN 9780231207225 (hardback)
ISBN 9780231207232 (trade paperback)
ISBN 9780231556873 (ebook)

LCCN: 2023013791

Printed in the United States of America

Cover image: Rajeev Lochan, *Reflection-Delhi 3*,
mixed media on silver gelatine print

For Robi
Remembering harmony

CONTENTS

PREFACE TO THE TWENTIETH ANNIVERSARY EDITION

TWENTY YEARS LATER

May CompLit rise again and again, sublated, in a relay, as long as the planet lasts. Comparative Literature, collectively embracing all the languages of the world, is the Humanities as such, beyond the disciplines, capable of keeping the academy internally practicing learning rather than simply acquiring and producing knowledge, and externally learning to learn from below.

A word about W. E. B. Du Bois before I begin. In the last twenty-odd years, between the first edition of *Death of a Discipline* and this second, I have been grappling with finishing a book on his life and work. In answer to a question asked by Brent Edwards on the more superficial version of Du Bois included in *Death of a Discipline*, I have written as follows: "About *Souls of Black Folk* I have much more to say and I have said them in that forthcoming book. That Du Bois claimed 'America' is incontrovertible. But to call it just 'nationalist,' as I did in the first edition, is unwise. And he was deeply critical of what we call 'identity politics,' of course."[1]

In 1999 I gave a talk at the Modern Language Association convention arranged by the American Comparative Literature Association. Jonathan Culler was in the audience and told me I should expand it and give it as the upcoming Wellek lectures, and so I did. I thanked him in the first edition, and I thank him again. He was right, the book seemed to fill a need. And most favorable readers seem to have liked the book because it appeared to offer a way to practice planetary readings.[2]

In 1997 I had proposed "planetarity" as a concept-metaphor to the Stiftung-Dialogik in Zurich.[3] It was there proposed as a limit to our powers. And yet it seems an enabler for *Death of a Discipline*, where I quote a bit from the Zurich piece.[4]

Let me quote from my entry on "planetarity" as it is to be found in Barbara Cassin's *Dictionary of the Untranslatables*, as translated by Emily Apter: "My use of 'planetarity' . . . does not refer to any applicable methodology. . . . Planetarity is not susceptible to the subject's grasp [*Begriff* = the German word for concept, containing the metaphor of grasp = *greifen*]."[5] And in this description, I give in conclusion the double bind of the ruse of consciousness, faced with the untranslatability of the word *planetarity*: "We must persistently educate ourselves into the peculiar mindset of accepting the untranslatable, even as we are programmed to transgress that mindset by 'translating' it into the mode of 'acceptance.'"

It is this "translation" that produces the reading practice welcomed by readers, mostly student readers. I finesse it by way of the uncanny, of figuration.

The method of *Death of a Discipline* can be fitted into my notion of "intended mistake." I have generally explained this emergence of method from the inaccessible by proposing a difference between the subject adrift in psycho-, historico-, politico-physical discontinuities (the planetary apart from even these) and agents validated by institutions, gender being the most encompassing, and, in the case of *Death of A Discipline*, for example, national education systems.

Today I would extend this by way of *die Vorstellung*, a German word notoriously difficult to translate. It is produced by *die Willkür*, an arbitrary need, rather than *die Wille*, which would lead you to the correct concept, of course. Today the need for a *willkürlich* (non)concept of planetarity is overwhelming. A totalizable theoretical correctness is not an option. The *Vorstellung* is contingent, dependent upon a methodological need.

In the *Economic and Philosophical Manuscripts*, for example, we see the recently doctorated well-trained young Marx moving from *Vorstellungen* to the irreducible, calling that end the concept. I cannot offer a detailed reading here for considerations of space and time, but I would like to suggest that this resolution is not achieved in the case of the important contradiction between species-life (*Gattungsleben*) and species-being (*Gattungswesen*). We take it so for granted that the young Karl Marx, humanist by inclination, should be clearly aiming for the best way for species-being to be equally accessible to one and all, that we do not notice how much more time he gives to species-life, and that, understanding and following Hegel of the *Phenomenology*, how much he mistrusts the human consciousness (which for Hegel can only harbor *Vorstellungen*), and that from the *Economic and Philosophical Manuscripts* (1843–44) all the way to

"The So-Called Primitive Accumulation," written twenty years later, Marx's sense of what we would call the Anthropocene is that it starts when human society is separated from self-consuming agriculture, separated from suckling Nature, as it were.[6] It is species-life that accumulation cannot catch, because there is no originary *Aneignung* or appropriation there.

As I argued in the eighties, Marx's predication of the human being is that it is super-adequate to itself, that it can make more than it needs.[7] This is the definitive predication of the historically developing subject of the Anthropocene. Today, offering this teacher's gift—a new *Death of a Discipline*—once again to my masters, my students—I would submit a reading of Christine Brooke-Rose's *Subscript*[8]—which begins with a scientifically correct representation of the contingent emergence of the eukaryotic cell—wthits—from out of thwi, their, as my Google research tells me. Husserl had given us the idea of the *Gegenständlich*, something that stands over against us, distinguishing it, as is the custom of German classical philosophy, from the Latin-origin *Objectivität*. Brooke-Rose's text starts with the eukaryote—the title of the first chapter is "Euka"—in the impossible first-philosophical task of representing the making of the human and therefore reading the irrational, as did Lacan in thinking the drives. The *Gegenstand* is before the narrative, not constitutable as the text's *Gegensatz* or contradiction; the text starts with the contingent, geobiological human material representing the planetary.

In the text, the reader shares the impossibility of perspectivizing this multiform, multicellular, pre-human perspective. The text's perspective is sometimes almost in the contemporary narrator's voice: Time "warmturns, lightturns, darkturns, foreverturns"—as long as things turn, the historical is not yet there. Through vague and repetitive mapmaking, much later, enter spatiality and the possibility of the historical. The akaryote is a "cell without a nucleus that has to depend on other organisms to survive." And the protagonist's name—representative of the human—is Aka (nickname for the akaryote?)—gradually becoming an individual, emerging into the narrative of Mesopotamia—literally, land "between two . . . rivers" (S 201), from where Aka's father receives a visitor—the historical start of a civilization of agriculture—by "dying" into the entire historical future, ending with "happily ever after." In Aka's dying fantastic vision combined with the real historiography of the future, we read, finally in achieved free indirect discourse:

> Then a horde of men with horse bodies and horse legs below them, shorter than the women because horses are stockier than bisons, come galloping after them, scattering seeds like rain with wide rainbow gestures into the loosened earth as they pass. And more and more, hordes and hordes of wheat-rearers and animal-tamers invading the huge forestless plain, the entire landmass, growing grains and greens and fruits and lambs and pigs and horses and having endless offspring and living happily ever after. (S 215)

The beginning of the Anthropocene. The human in excess of herself, seeds sprouting. Species-life coming to an end at the remote origin of primitive accumulation.

"Happily ever after" echoes the same phrase occurring earlier in the text when the originary "we" emerges possibly in the rainforest of the Amazon (S 73): "we have been for ever"—this leads to the difficulty of representing time in the text—"in this rich rainy forest and live happily ever after." The reader might notice the divergence in tenses in the sentence once again signaling the difficulty of historical representation, now in the emerging human subject collectively female, which was already indicated on page 57, where the as-yet-undifferentiated "subject" says: "so the original division of labor between male and female has become even more unequal." To have the originary human subject as female is "logical," for, by the code, "the pack's [later the "group's," "tribe's"] sole duty is to survive, and replicate," a formula repeated many many times in the text. I like to think that the impersonality or generality of the gendered subject can also be read as proper name/common noun—Aka— "also known as"—all of us?

There is a reading of Mahasweta Devi's exquisite "Pterodactyl" in the first edition. I add a bit of reading that had not come to me until the times changed into a pervasive recall to planetarity: in the first edition we had not noticed that Mahasweta distinguishes between extinction by planetarity and anthropocentric extinction as imagined by Puran trying to "read" what the pterodactyl's message might be. The first sentence is about planetarity. The rest about our responsibility for killing our earth: "We are extinct by the inevitable natural geological evolution. You too are endangered. You too will become extinct in nuclear explosions, or in war, or in the aggressive advance of the strong obliterating the weak, which finally turns you naked, barbaric, primitive" (157–158). The story is necessarily stylized, romanticizing the indigenous as it achieves the remote settler colonial's "excruciating" love (196) within the powerful concept-metaphor of bringing the map alive.

To Devi's text I would add Marguerite Duras's mysterious *Sea Wall*, published in 1950, when the awareness of planetarity had not been politically correct for smart capitalism.[9] To point out how irresponsible this translation is, I would quote this passage from my own recent writing:

May translating rather than translation be the future of the humanities. We will be a global community, each one of us globalizable, upstream from politics, an island of languaging in a field of traces. The trace of an "unknown" language is where we know meaningfulness is operating, but we don't know how. Our task as teachers and translators calls us into this challenge, the recognition that a fully translated globe is nothing that we should desire. . . . The final project of translating is an epistemological project upon ourselves, like all translation, necessary but impossible. Post colonial was focused on the nation state. To supplement globalization, we need archipelago-thought. Edouard Glissant, the thinker of creolity, has said: "Translation is therefore one of the most important kinds of this new archipelagic thinking."[10] We must displace the heritage of postcoloniality into island-thinking. [Viet Nam] can move into this with brilliance. We are all islanders.[11]

Duras's text prefigures this move by way of a spirit turned by what she calls the "native colonials," "the whites who had made no fortune," and the translation misses this on every page. The comparative literary impulse reads translation translating; and notices that the echo of the sea—"la mer"—every time the book refers to the mother—the main character—as the generic unappropriated "la mère"—would be missed in English, even if it had translated the word generically rather than with the completely inappropriate "Ma." Learn French, the French book says. Only then can we suspect that—in this text—the Anthropocene acts out the baseline human, as the sea acts out its program of destruction. This female native colonial—the mother turned by life—is staged as the baseline human. We begin to see that the book tabulates its characters in terms of their relationship to this unheroic version of planetarity, the other term being class. The most moving class-tabulated character detail being the Corporal's (affectionate name, like *capitano* in Latin New York City, for an illiterate deaf Malay servant with a family) to identify his own poverty with the mother's, although he knows she is poor and cannot pay him.

The third term of character tabulation in *A Barrier Against the Pacific* (which is the literal translation of the title) is gender. Unlike in Brooke-Rose and Devi, this is an extramoral assessment of gender as the instrument of class-mobility as well as impermanent productive joy.[12] It is Venn diagrammed with a sustained description of the ceaseless fecundity of peasant women, a description that forbids the reader to counterfocalize by its absolute and monotonous resistance even to free indirect discourse.[13] We must rather imagine this peculiar description extramorally, not quite knowing how to put it in the book's mode of production of value, of intellectual capital. The text has informed us that the children are fed chewed food by their mothers by mouth-to-mouth transfer, as are birds, and that they are covered with a saffron powder over nakedness to avoid malaria, that the tigers will not eat them because the tigers are not hungry!

The children offer a clue at the end of the book. The mother is dead, and everyone is about to depart, hither and yon, the son as half of a class-hypergamous couple. The closure of the book claims a solemn voice through a somewhat erratic intermittent and interruptive use of the French *passé simple* form here and there, mingled with the mundane imperfect. And right at the end, the children remain, making noise, just noise: "One heard their soft cheeping [*piaillements*] come out of the spaces [*sortir des cases*]."[14]

If you want human beings in a "common measure" (SW 197; translation modified) with located planetarity, the ocean eating the ground with a programmed regularity, here they are, with only a natural future, contingent as human. "No hungry generations tread [them] down."[15] Nature is these children's "inorganic body."[16]

Some years after *Death of a Discipline* I published *Readings*, addressed to English majors and post-tertiary scholars of English in India.[17] But more recently I have been able to connect subalternity with a task for Comparative Literature.

"Pterodactyl" shows us the map coming alive. *A Barrier Against the Pacific* shows us the mother (*la mère*) punned with the sea (*la mer*). A peculiar passage in the book emphasizes this odd coupling, puts the children on the map even as it does not:

What the children died of in the marshy plains of Kam, enclosed on one side by the China Sea—which the mother obstinately called the Pacific, "China Sea" having in her eyes something provincial, and because, when she was young, it was to the Pacific ocean that she had reported her dreams and not to any of those small seas that uselessly complicate things—and walled in toward the East by the very long chain which ranged the coast from very high up in the Asiatic continent, following a descending curve to the Gulf of Siam where it submerged and reappeared . . . (SW 24–25; translation modified)

Placing the children in the one water of the world, misnamed "pacific," as it destroys human work and eats the land.

These passages resonated with a sense of new tasks for elite and subaltern that had come to me as a result of the sense of the climate disaster already upon us. Asked by New York's Asia Society to reimagine the museum, I had said:

Let me confront [my] mother's liberalism, well-inherited by me: as acknowledgment of complicity (being folded together with what I critique), I have tried to use deconstruction as affirmative sabotage: do not excuse (saying "art can heal"), do not accuse (saying "museum is colonial"), but—enter that social formation that you are criticizing as thoroughly as you can (among our hosts this is not a problem, they are deeply and authoritatively imbricated in the curatorial work, it is a powerful auto critique)—so, enter to find in it a toehold that will allow you to turn the whole thing around to serve purposes other than its original self-comprehension. The sexy name for this toehold is "the moment of transgression." The pioneering introduction of land acknowledgments into the Metropolitan Museum allowed me such a toehold—the walls of the museum were transgressed or breached. The walls of the museum of the metropolis, *the* metropolis, had been breached, it has been located as mere built space. Let us listen to Mieke Bal on the Met:

The Met fits all the priorities of its own social environment: Western European art dominates, American art is represented as a good second cousin, evolving as Europe declines, while the parallel marginal treatment of "archaic" and "foreign" art, from Mesopotamian to Indian, contrasts with the importance accorded to "ancient" as predecessor: the Greeks and Romans. As "natural" as such priorities may seem—due to what is available, one might say; but why? the difference with the British Museum in this respect tells us that these random facts are not so arbitrary. The overall impression is one of complete control, possession, storage: the Met has the art of the world within its walls, and its visitors have it in their pocket. It is possible to attribute this odd combination to the racism inherent in the colonialist origin of the museum, safely referred back to an age before today's alleged race and gender consciousness.

Bal's piece was published in 1992. The Met has made many conscientious changes since then, as it has passed through different directorships. Yet it must nonetheless be said that it might not be enough to appoint the brilliant new Associate Curator, Patricia Marroquin Norby, Purépecha, and to "include Native American objects" now defined as "art."

Let us read the acknowledgment, necessarily in English.

"The Metropolitan Museum of Art is situated in Lenapehoking, homeland of the Lenape diaspora, and historically a gathering and trading place for many diverse native peoples, who continue to live and work on this island. We respectfully acknowledge and honor all Indigenous communities—past, present, and future—for their ongoing and fundamental relationships to the region."

The Lenapes, like subaltern Africans, were multilingual, and Lenape itself is, like Yoruba, a collective singular name for a multiplicity. What is it simply to say: we are sitting on your land but we respect you? I am not speaking of open-air museums, Yosemite, etc. Not

THE METROPOLITAN MUSEUM OF ART
IS SITUATED IN LENAPEHOKING,
HOMELAND OF THE LENAPE DIASPORA,
AND HISTORICALLY A GATHERING AND
TRADING PLACE FOR MANY DIVERSE
NATIVE PEOPLES, WHO CONTINUE TO
LIVE AND WORK ON THIS ISLAND.

WE RESPECTFULLY ACKNOWLEDGE
AND HONOR ALL INDIGENOUS
COMMUNITIES—PAST, PRESENT, AND
FUTURE—FOR THEIR ONGOING
AND FUNDAMENTAL RELATIONSHIPS
TO THE REGION.

Bronze plaque installed on the facade of the Metropolitan Museum of Art, Fifth Avenue facade. It is placed below a similar plaque that pays tribute to the City of New York.

of creating the artificial natural. I am reminding you that at the end of *Capital*, vol. 1, Karl Marx suggests that the capitalization (read spectralization-museumization) of land produces so-called primitive accumulation, making industrial capitalism possible. Thus, allowing the "Native American" the same modernity as ourselves, in today's contested future, rather than propose "sustainable tourism" (I quote the World Monuments Heritage Fund), we should all learn to undo our minds to realize that (ourselves as) the world itself—and this is everyone—can only acknowledge that it was imposed on commons. For this, one of our tasks (indicated by suggestions, for example, to the World Economic Forum and Comparative Education Society), is to impart to the subaltern indigenous a real sense of the cartographic world, rather than dwell on the fact that most indigenous languages have a word for "world," but not for "colonialism," or "deconstruction."

How is this tremendous epistemological performance, sustained by imaginative activism rather than cost-effectiveness, to be achieved? Perhaps it will hit us by creative chance (Aristotle calls this *tuchè*) as we perform the short-term tasks assiduously, without personal politics; or, bigger yet, let us turn to the . . . mad mathematician/philosopher Ludwig Wittgenstein: "when we arbitrarily conceptualize something . . . we are not surprised by those *Vorstellungen* enough to say 'Look there!' " (trans. modified). We must wait for the re-imagined meta-museality as dictated by the planetary to surprise us.[18]

This surprise, at the contingent rather than the expected necessary breaking in upon us, is the quality of the literary. And the literary "translates" the planetary—the meta-museal geobiological—into contingency.

In the long passage, the task for the elite and the subaltern are differentiated as follows. I repeat:

Thus, allowing the "Native American" the same modernity as ourselves, in today's contested future, rather than propose "sustainable tourism" (I quote the World Monuments Heritage Fund), we should all learn to undo our minds to realize that (ourselves as) *the world itself—and this is everyone—can only acknowledge that it was imposed on commons.* For this, one of our tasks (indicated by suggestions, for example, to the World

Economic Forum and Comparative Education Society), is to *impart to the subaltern indigenous a real sense of the cartographic world*, rather than dwell on the fact that most indigenous languages have a word for "world," but not for "colonialism," or "deconstruction."

Comparative Literature must work out the details on the repeated relay of the performance of these tasks in terms of specific historical social relations of the production of value. Let me cite here a welcome local effort undertaken with my beloved colleague Rosalind Carmel Morris. It is to record bits of television or social media programs explanatory of climate disasters that would be accessible to the cognitive preparation of specific subaltern groups that we have associated with, learning to learn from below; and get them subtitled in the world's wealth of subaltern languages. We would still not be able to access the unsystematized languages, and also not the vast population, the major victims of the Anthropocene, who use mnemic languages—languages written on memory—generally described as illiterate. How to undermine top-down philanthropy in this performance? Another task for Comparative Literature beyond the disciplines. I am trying to find an answer to this, but cannot talk about it yet.[19]

Some years ago, I reopened an unfinished conversation with Derrida, interrogating his suggestion that followable directions within a forest—the prefiguration of mapmaking—was the first writing. My thoughts ultimately became "Halting the Map Maker," Inaugural Lecture, 50th Annual Convention, International Association of Art Critics, Paris, November 13, 2017. I have not been able to publish the lecture because my subject there is the feminine transcendental, and, like (but of course nothing is "like" planetarity, the "just[ice] of the weather," as *Beloved* will have it) planetarity, we cannot grasp it, but bits and pieces are here and there.[20] The feminine transcendental, graspable only through the structure of marriage, is absorbed into the Earth in conclusion. In the first edition, I read Diamela Eltit, who formed part of a course, twenty years ago, when I was edging toward thinking the feminine transcendental, and had come as far as the impossibility of representing a feminist hero. Zoë Wicomb's *David's Story* was part of the syllabus.[21] Gender remains the dangerous supplement, wedging the incalculable into the totality of any system, even of Comparative Literature beyond the disciplines. So I stand here on the margins of your book, in the name of the incalculable and the untranslatable, and say to the reader, grab the baton and run, take it somewhere else, as long as the planet lasts.

NOTES

1. Gayatri Chakravorty Spivak, "To My Questioners· Alphabetically Listed by Last Name," *Comparative Literature Studies* 60, no. 2 (May 2023). This interview in *Comparative Literary Studies* is published as part of a forum titled "Traveling with *Death of a Discipline*: Forum on the Twentieth Anniversary of the Publication of *Death of a Discipline*." I also ask my readers to glance at my book on Du Bois, tentatively entitled *My Brother Burghardt*, forthcoming from Harvard University Press.

2. For an account of the production of knowledge on the occasion of planetarity, see Dipesh Chakrabarty, *Climate of History in A Planetary Age* (Chicago: University of Chicago Press, 2021) and its voluminous documentation. He does not, of course, think of the humanities as training in the practice of learning, but rather, contrasts them to science as follows: "Every consensus in the sciences exists only to be challenged by new research, which is why consensuses are much harder won than in the humanities, which in contrast and by its very nature often seems to be a collection of schismatic churches and their conflicting dogma" ("Planetary Humanities: Straddling the Decolonial/Postcolonial Divide," *Daedalus* 151 [3] [Summer 2022]: 230). He contrasts the "findings and propositions of Earth system science, [where] the climate crisis becomes a human encounter with the idea of ourselves as a geological

force, an encounter, that is, both with geological deep time and with our entanglement with other forms of life and thus with the geobiological history of the planet." In response to this, he sees "humanists"—by which I suppose he also means humanities teachers—as "constant[ly] invoking . . . a potential *we* of humans as part of conditional solution-proposing statements that take the form of 'If only we . . .'" (230–231). As I will argue in this preface, our *we* must always remain ready for expansion, and change form, keeping the idea of the collectivity related to our work as "relay," by way of something like the dispersed "new international" of which Derrida wrote many years ago (Spivak, "A Note on the New International," *parallax* 20 [July–September 2001]: 12–16). Although I share Chakrabarty's view that the conformity of indigenous groups to their own cultural prescriptions, often more fearful of "Nature" because of technological simplicity, should not be confused with environmentalism and is not going to lead directly to solutions to the climate crisis without massive epistemic intervention, I do think that there are mythic signals for thinking something like deep history and the geobiological in their cultural formation. As I suggest on pages 72–73 of the first edition, "We provide for ourselves transcendental figurations of what we think is the origin of this animating gift of animation, if there is any: Mother, Nation, God, Nature. These are names of alterity, some more radical than others. Planet-thought opens up to embrace an inexhaustible taxonomy of the whole range of human universals: including but not identical with aboriginal animism as well as the spectral white mythology of post-rational science." Keeping herself to the literary, Thangam Ravindranathan has suggested that we read passages that seem to signal toward such mythic hints toward deep history and the geobiological with something like superstition ("Superstitious Reading," paper presented at the conference, "Climate Crisis in South Asia: Imagining Other Ways," Columbia University, October 14, 2022). As I have argued elsewhere, the contingent escapes all production of knowledge. With Wittgenstein, I suggest keeping the door open for the contingent through the idea of being surprised by alterity "translated" into the contingent. The idea will be explored further in the text (see pages 17, 23, and passim).

3. Initially published in both English and German as *Imperatives to Re-Imagine the Planet / Imperative zur Neuerfindung des Planeten*, ed. Willi Goetschel (Vienna: Passagen, 1999). Reprinted in a revised version as "Imperative to Re-Imagine the Planet," in Spivak, *An Aesthetic Education*

in the Era of Globalization (Cambridge, MA: Harvard University Press, 2012), 335–350.

4. Gayatri Chakravorty Spivak, *Death of a Discipline* (New York: Columbia University Press, 2003), 33 and 86. Hereafter cited in the text with page reference alone.

5. Gayatri Chakravorty Spivak, "Planetarity," in Barbara Cassin, ed., *Dictionary of Untranslatables: A Philosophical Lexicon* (Princeton, NJ: Princeton University Press, 2014), 1223.

6. "So-Called Primitive Accumulation," in Karl Marx, *Capital*, vol. 1, *A Critique of Political Economy*, tr. Ben Fowkes (London: Penguin, 1976), 873–942.

7. Gayatri Chakravorty Spivak, "Scattered Speculations on the Question of Value," *Diacritics* 15 (4) (Winter 1985): 73–93.

8. Christine Brooke-Rose, *Subscript* (Manchester: Carcanet, 1999); hereafter cited in the text as S, followed by page reference.

9. Marguerite Duras, *Sea Wall* (London: Faber, 1986), 138 (translation modified); hereafter cited in the text as SW, followed by page reference.

10. Édouard Glissant, *Introduction to a Poetics of Diversity*, tr. Celia Britton (Liverpool: Liverpool University Press, [1996] 2020), 27.

11. Spivak, "How the Heritage of Postcolonial Studies Thinks Colonialism Today," *Janus Unbound* 1 (1) (Fall 2021): 26–27.

12. Extramoral in the sense of Nietzsche's "Truth and Lie in an Extra-Moral Sense," in *The Birth of Tragedy and Other Writings*, tr. Ronald Speirs (Cambridge: Cambridge University Press, 1999), 139–153.

13. For a discussion of how textual rhetoric calls for counterfocalization, see my reading of J. M. Coetzee's *Disgrace* in "Ethics and Politics in Tagore, Coetzee, and Certain Scenes of Teaching," in Spivak, *Aesthetic Education*, 316–334. Gerald Prince's warning, given to me in private conversation, that free indirect discourse recognition depends upon the reader must be kept in mind. It can produce the kind of politically correct reading as the African National Congress's dismissal of *Disgrace* as racist.

14. SW 288; translation modified. The English makes them "babble"—humanizing—and translates *cases* as "cabins," socializing. Earlier (SW 25) *piailler* is translated as "cheeping," as the noise the children make.

15. This is how John Keats celebrated the sameness of creatures of natural origin, contrasting it with the differentiated lives and deaths of

individuated human beings in "Ode to a Nightingale." In Duras's unrelenting fictive world, these children are represented in that sameness. The translation does not preserve the rhetoric that signals this to the canny reader.

16. Karl Marx, "Economic and Philosophical Manuscripts," in *Early Writings*, tr. Gregor Benton (New York: Vintage, 1975), 328.

17. Gayatri Chakravorty Spivak, *Readings* (Calcutta: Seagull, 2014).

18. Please consult Vijay Prashad, "In the Name of Saving the Climate They Will Uberise the Farmland: The Forty-Sixth Newsletter (2021)," Tricontinental: Institute for Social Research, for an example of the spectralization of land. Examples are everywhere. https://thetricontinental.org/newsletterissue/agricultural-technology/.

19. Work started with Oluwaseun Akinfenwa.

20. Especially in the memorial tribute to Nabaneeta Dev Sen ("A Tribute to the Incomparable," Nabaneeta Dev Sen Memorial Lecture, January 15, 2022). I have also been unable to publish a piece relating to the feminine transcendental, "Imagination, Not Culture: A Singular Example," William James Lecture, Harvard Divinity School, April 10, 2008.

21. Zoë Wicomb, *David's Story* (New York: Feminist Press, 2001).

ACKNOWLEDGMENTS

I am grateful to Jonathan Culler for having suggested that I choose this subject for my Wellek Library Lectures. It is a subject that has been close to my heart since I became Chair of Comparative Literature at the University of Iowa in 1975. That was an enlightened university, where a young chair was allowed to experiment with her odd ideas about building a discipline. My next chance to explore the topic came in 1986, at the University of Pittsburgh, with the founding of the Institute for Cultural Studies. The Center for Comparative Literature and Society at Columbia reflects every lesson learned at Iowa and Pittsburgh.

Between the presentation of the lectures in May 2000 and the final revision in May 2002, the discipline of comparative literature in the United States underwent a sea change. Publishing conglomerates have recognized a market for anthologies of world literature in translation. Academics with large advances are busy putting these together. Typically, the entire literature of China, say, is represented by a couple of chapters of *The Dream of the Red Chamber* and a few pages of poetry. Notes and introduction are provided by a scholar from the area commissioned for the purpose by the general editor, located in the United States. The market is international. Students in Taiwan or Nigeria will learn about the literatures of the world through English translations organized by the United States. Thus institutionalized, this global education market will need teachers. Presumably, the graduate discipline of comparative literature will train those teachers.

The book you are about to read is therefore out of joint with the times in a more serious way than the Wellek Library Lectures of May 2000 were. I have changed nothing of the urgency of my call for "a new comparative literature." I hope the book will be read as the last gasp of a dying discipline.

A gasp is better than silence. One can write in the hope that there may be some in the academy who do not believe that the critical edge of the humanities should be appropriated and determined by the market. Perhaps not immediately—but one of these days? Let the ghost dance.

Henry Staten has been a wonderful first reader, inspiring a thorough revision. Whatever faults remain are mine.

DEATH OF A DISCIPLINE

CHAPTER 1

CROSSING BORDERS

Since 1992, three years after the fall of the Berlin Wall, the discipline of comparative literature has been looking to renovate itself. This is presumably in response to the rising tide of multiculturalism and cultural studies. The first pages of Charles Bernheimer's *Comparative Literature in the Age of Multiculturalism* tell a story that those with experience of national-level professional organizations at work can flesh out in the imagination into a version of the Quarrel of the Ancients and the Moderns:

In the summer of 1992 . . . [the] president of the American Comparative Literature Association (ACLA), asked me to appoint and chair a committee charged to write a so-called Report on Standards for submission to the association. The bylaws of the ACLA . . . mandated that such a report be prepared every ten years. The first report was submitted in 1965 by a committee chaired by my thesis director, Harry Levin; the second was submitted in 1975 by a committee chaired by Tom Greene. A third report was written ten years thereafter, but . . . the chair of that committee was so dissatisfied with the document that he exercised a pocket veto and never submitted it. . . . The first two reports . . . are impressively strong articulations of a view of comparative literature which, in my view, no longer applies to actual practices in the field. . . . A diverse group of top scholars from diverse institutions . . . felt uneasy about being asked to establish "standards" and decided to give more importance to our ideas about the intellectual mission of the discipline than to spelling out requirements (. . . the report [was renamed] the Report on the State of the Discipline).[1]

This is an account of the transformation of comparative literary studies. Comparative social studies, as represented by Area Studies, were undergoing their own transformation. This is well represented by a recent influential pamphlet by Toby Volkman, written while she was Program Officer at the Ford Foundation, from which I have taken my chapter title: "Crossing Borders":

Recent developments have challenged some of the premises of area studies itself. The notion, for example, that the world can be divided into knowable, self-contained "areas" has come into question as more attention has been paid to movements between areas. Demographic shifts, diasporas, labor migrations, the movements of global capital and media, and processes of cultural circulation and hybridization have encouraged a more subtle and sensitive reading of areas' identity and composition.[2]

The rest of Volkman's pamphlet contains actual descriptions of institutional projects under six headings: Reconceptualization of "Area"; Borders and Diasporas; Border-Crossing Seminars and Workshops; Curricular Transformation and Integration; Collaborations with Nongovernmental Organizations, Activists, and the Media; and Rethinking Scientific Areas. There are a few examples of Ethnic Studies and Area Studies pulling together, but the only one that may touch traditional comparative literature is the project at Middlebury College, building on its already considerable resources of European language teaching. Indeed, although "popular culture" is an item often included, literature does not seem particularly important in this venture of, as Volkman's subtitle suggests, "Revitalizing Area Studies."[3]

If this is what may be called the current situation, the recent past of these two institutional enterprises can perhaps be recounted as follows. Area Studies were established to secure U.S. power in the Cold War. Comparative Literature was a result of European intellectuals fleeing "totalitarian" regimes. Cultural and Postcolonial Studies relate to the 500 percent increase in Asian immigration in the wake of Lyndon Johnson's reform of the Immigration Act of 1965. Whatever our view of what we do, we are made by the forces of people moving about the world.

How can we respond to the changes brought about by the end of the Cold War, as both the Bernheimer report and the Volkman pamphlet implicitly ask? A simple splicing of Comp. Lit. and Cultural Studies/multiculturalism will not work or will work only too well; same difference. A combination of Ethnic Studies and Area Studies bypasses the literary and the linguistic. What I am proposing is not a politicization of the discipline. We are *in* politics. I am proposing an attempt to depoliticize in order to move away from a politics of hostility, fear, and half solutions. Why, for example, as in the fairly representative passage below, appropriate Brecht to trash Ethnic Studies and Cultural Studies in order to praise a friend's book in the pages of a journal that was established in 1949, in the full flush of Area Studies development, "at a time when the strengthening of good international relations [was] of paramount importance"?

> In the face of the wholesale selling-off of the German intellectual tradition by current "German Studies" and the shallowing of philosophically-informed literary theory by the conversion of comparative literature into cultural studies, *Premises* brings to mind Brecht's 1941 comment on Benjamin's "Theses on the Philosophy of History": "one thinks with horror of how small the number is of those who are ready even to misunderstand something like this."[4]

Compared to such an outburst, my ideas for an inclusive comparative literature are so depoliticized as to have, unlike the Bernheimer report or the Volkman pamphlet, little to do with the times. I thought Comparative Literature should be world embracing at the beginning of my career. And I continue to believe that the politics of the production of knowledge in area studies (and also anthropology and the other "human sciences") can be touched by a new Comparative Literature, whose hallmark remains a care for language and idiom.

In 1973, when I was an associate professor, I invited Claudio Guillén to the University of Iowa to give a minicourse. Guillén was moved by my idealism about a global Comparative Literature. He put me on the Executive Committee of the International Comparative Literature Association. I went to Visegrad the following year. I wish I could regale the reader with the symptomatology of that meeting, but must confine myself to one detail.

The association was putting together new scholarly volumes on the periods of European literary history. We discussed the production details of the volume on the Renaissance, if memory serves. I offered to get contacts for scholars in the Indian languages so that we could enlarge the scope of the series. I offered to be active in setting up committees for such investigations in the other comparative clusters of the world: Korean–Chinese–Japanese; Arabic–Persian; the languages of Southeast Asia; African languages. A foolish notion, no doubt. M. Voisine of the Sorbonne, a senior member of the committee, quelled me with a glance: "My friend René Etiemble tells me," he said, "that there is a perfectly acceptable scholarly history of literatures in Chinese."

Memory has no doubt sharpened the exchange. And one person's caustic remark cannot represent an entire discipline. What the exchange does vouch for, however, is my longstanding sense that the logical consequences of our loosely defined discipline were, surely, to include the open-ended possibility of studying all literatures, with linguistic rigor and historical savvy. A level playing field, so to speak.

As it happened, I had also been speaking of what was not yet called Cultural Studies teaming up with Area Studies for some time. Selecting one example among many, I quote myself, admonishing, in 1988: "As we in the margins try to shore up our defenses, we tend to leave untouched the politics of the specialists of the margin—area studies, anthropology, and the like."[5]

Even from a restricted U.S. perspective, it seems obvious that the sources of literary agency have expanded beyond the old European national literatures. For the *discipline*, the way out seems to be to acknowledge a definitive future anteriority, a "to come"-ness, a "will have happened" quality. This is a protection from self-destructive competition for dwindling resources. It is also a protection from losing the best of the old Comparative Literature: the skill of reading closely in the original. Such a philosophy of planning welcomes nonexhaustive taxonomies, provisional system making, but discourages mapmaking literary criticism as an end in itself because diagnostic cartography does not keep the door open to the "to come." It is in the acknowledgment of such an open future that we need to consider the resources of Area Studies, specifically geared for what lies beyond the Euro–U.S.

In spite of all the noise about "these times," if the 145 departments or programs listed in the bulletin of the ACLA form a representative sample, the general model in Comparative Literature seemed still, in 2000 when these lectures were delivered, to be Europe and the extracurricular Orient. Ten Comp. Lit. units in the United States seem to have some arrangement with either the social sciences or multiculturalism, and only two of these mention Area Studies. I have no doubt that this is now changing, but cannot keep up with the pace of that change.

Area Studies were founded in the wake of the Cold War and funded by federal grants, backed up by the great foundations, especially Ford.

To meet the demands of war, scholars of diverse disciplines *were forced* to pool their knowledge in frantic attempts to advise administrators and policy makers.... The war also showed the need for trained personnel for most foreign areas. ... In these Army Specialized Training Programs and Civil Affairs Training Schools many professors had their first experience with curricula organized by area rather than by discipline, and many students made a real beginning in the study of foreign areas and in their languages,

says the introduction to the "national conference on the study of world areas, which was held in New York on November 28–30, 1947."[6] Language and Area Centers between 1959 and 1968 were authorized by Public Law 85–864, the National Defense Education Act of 1958 (as amended), Title VI.

Without the support of the humanities, Area Studies can still only transgress frontiers, in the name of crossing borders; and, without a transformed Area Studies, Comparative Literature remains imprisoned within the borders it will not cross. Area studies have resources but also built-in, restricted, but real interdisciplinarity. If one goes down the list of Comparative Literature programs and departments, the interdisciplinarity with music, philosophy, art history, and media remains less persuasive and exceptional. And, whatever we think about the relationship between Comparative Literature and Area Studies, the polarity between Area Studies and Cultural Studies is clear.

Area Studies exhibit quality and rigor (those elusive traits), combined with openly conservative or "no" politics. They are tied to the politics of power, and their connections to the power elite in the countries studied are still strong; the quality of the language learning is generally excellent, though just as generally confined to the needs of social science fieldwork; and the data processing is sophisticated, extensive, and intensive. Academic "Cultural Studies," as a metropolitan phenomenon originating on the radical fringes of national language departments, opposes this with no more than metropolitan language–based presentist and personalist political convictions, often with visibly foregone conclusions that cannot match the implicit political cunning of Area Studies at their best; and earns itself a reputation for "lack of rigor" as well as for politicizing the academy.[7] The languages of the cultures of origin are invoked at best as delexicalized and fun mother tongues. The real "other" of Cultural Studies is not Area Studies but the civilization courses offered by the European national language departments, generally scorned by Comparative Literature. It is therefore a real sign of change that the Ford initiative, as reflected in the Volkman pamphlet, seems to bring together Ethnic/Cultural Studies and Area Studies. It remains to be seen if the extraordinary metropolitan enthusiasm in the former will undermine the linguistic rigor of the latter. I will discuss that question in the last chapter. Let us return to Comparative Literature.

Area Studies related to foreign "areas." Comparative Literature was made up of Western European "nations." This distinction, between "areas" and "nations," infected Comparative Literature from the start.[8]

If the "origin" of Area Studies was the aftermath of the Cold War, the "origin" of U.S. Comparative Literature had something of a relationship with the events that secured it: the flights of European intellectuals, including such distinguished men as Erich Auerbach, Leo Spitzer, René Wellek, Renato Poggioli, and Claudio Guillén, from "totalitarian" regimes in Europe. One might say that U.S. Comparative Literature was founded on inter-European hospitality, even as Area Studies had been spawned by interregional vigilance.

One way that the nation-region divide is already being negotiated in comparative literature is by destabilizing the "nation"(s)—introducing Francophony, Teutophony, Lusophony, Anglophony, Hispanophony within the old "national" boundaries; the biggest winner in the United States is "Global English." The effort, recalling the initial Birmingham model of Cultural Studies, is to put some black on the Union Jack or, to put a spin on Jesse Jackson's slogan, to paint the red, white, and blue in the colors of the rainbow.[9] This destabilization follows the lines of the old imperialisms and competes with the diversified metropolitan nationalism of Ethnic/Cultural Studies.

The new step that I am proposing would go beyond this acknowledgment and this competition. It would work to make the traditional linguistic sophistication of Comparative Literature supplement Area Studies (and history, anthropology, political theory, and sociology) by approaching the language of the other not only as a "field" language. In the field of literature, we need to move from Anglophony, Lusophony, Teutophony, Francophony, et cetera. We must take the languages of the Southern Hemisphere as active cultural media rather than as objects of cultural study by the sanctioned ignorance of the metropolitan migrant. We cannot dictate a model for this from the offices of the American Comparative Literature Association. We can, however, qualify ourselves and our students to attend upon this as it happens elsewhere. Here and now, I can only caution against some stereotypes: that such an interest is antihybridist, culturally conservative, "ontopologist," "parochial."[10] Indeed, I am inviting the kind of language training that would disclose the irreducible hybridity of all languages. As I have said elsewhere: "The verbal text is jealous of its linguistic signature but impatient of national identity. Translation flourishes by virtue of that paradox."[11] Other stereotypes are correct but irrelevant: namely, that attention to the languages of the Southern Hemisphere is inconvenient and impractical.[12]

Inconvenient. There are a few hegemonic European languages and innumerable Southern Hemisphere languages. The only principled answer to that is: "Too bad." The old Comparative Literature did not ask the student to learn every hegemonic language; nor will the new ask her or him to learn all the subaltern ones! Can the "native informant" ever become the subject of a "cultural study" that does not resemble metropolitan language–based work? If one asks this question, one sees that the destabilization offered by a merely metropolitan Cultural Studies must exclude much for its own convenience, for the cultural claims of the metropolitan migrant.

Jacques Derrida is the rare philosopher who thinks that philosophical "concepts [cannot] transcend idiomatic differences."[13] Such insights do not apply only to French and German or Greek and Latin. Engagement with the idiom of the global other(s) in the Southern Hemisphere, uninstitutionalized in the Euro–U.S. university structure except via the objectifying, discontinuous, transcoding tourist gaze of anthropology and oral history, is our lesson on displacing the discipline. This is not brought about by the reterritorialized desire of the metropolitan migrant to collaborate with the South, generally through the United Nations by way of nongovernmental organizations (NGOs). As I have argued elsewhere, such collaboration is generally possible only with the class, physically "based" in the global South, increasingly produced by globalization, that is sufficiently out of touch with the idiomaticity of nonhegemonic languages.[14]

What I am suggesting may sound discouraging. I hate to use this word, but perhaps it gives us a certain kind of honesty. It should not paralyze us. We cannot not try to open up, from the inside, the colonialism of European national language–based

Comparative Literature and the Cold War format of Area Studies, and infect history and anthropology with the "other" as producer of knowledge. From the inside, acknowledging complicity. No accusations. No excuses. Rather, learning the protocol of those disciplines, turning them around, laboriously, not only by building institutional bridges but also by persistent curricular interventions. The most difficult thing here is to resist mere appropriation by the dominant.[15]

Indeed, the question of the old imperialisms and the new empire is itself different if uncoupled from high-culture radicalism. While I was working on this manuscript, I was also looking at the *Report of the Mayor's Task Force on the City University of New York*, undertaken in 1998.[16] The question before us was "What is English? Literary Studies in a Public Urban University." The City University of New York was faulted because 87 percent of its incoming undergraduate class was in remedial English. The report separated the old minorities—giving them the code name of New York City public school graduates—from the new—emergent since Lyndon Johnson lifted the quota system in 1965: "During the 1990's, the white population of New York City declined by 19.3%, while the black, Hispanic, and Asian population have risen by 5.2%, 19.3%, and 53.5%, respectively."

If you sit in on these so-called remedial classes, you perceive the institutional incapacity to cope with the crossroads of race, gender and class—even when the teacher has the best will in the world—to come to grips with the actual play of the choice of English as tongue in the imagination of these working-class new immigrant survival artists. *Le Thé Au Harem d'Archi Ahmed.*[17] As a comparativist I would like to suggest that, just as no "literary studies" in New York City and no doubt in Los Angeles should forget that the answer to the question "What is English?" is that it is more than half the ingredient for producing human capital (the other half being mathematics), so also, literary studies will have to acknowledge that the European outlines of its premise and one of its tasks—positing the idea of the universality of each of the European national languages (the jealously guarded particular domain of the old Comparative Literature)—have, in globality and in subaltern U.S. multiculturalism, altogether disappeared. There are Haitians and West Africans in those CUNY remedial classes whose imaginations are crossing and being crossed by a double aporia—the cusp of two imperialisms. I have learned something from listening to their talk about and in Creole/French/so-called pidgin and English-as-a-second-language-crossing-into-first—the chosen tongue. I have silently compared their imaginative flexibility, so remarkably and necessarily much stronger, because constantly in use for social survival and mobility, than that of the Columbia undergraduate, held up by the life-support system of a commercializing anglophone culture that trivializes the humanities. It is time, in globality, in New York, and no doubt elsewhere in the metropolis, to put the history of Francophony, Teutophony, Lusophony, Anglophony, Hispanophony *also*—not *only* (please mark the difference)—in a comparative focus.

To pursue this line of thinking further would be to address the question of the thickening of class analysis itself and would take us away from the question of Comparative Literature. I place this parenthesis here so that the reader will take this postponement into account.

Outside of "Gender and Development," the question of human rights is most often confined within trade-related political paradigms leading to military intervention, ostensibly based on game theory and rational choice as unacknowledged theoretical models. If a responsible comparativism can be of the remotest possible use in the training of the imagination, it must approach culturally diversified ethical systems diachronically, through the history of multicultural empires, without foregone conclusions. This is the material that is used to fashion violence in the multiform global imaginary. Pedagogically speaking, such studies are much more successful through language-based literary investigation than through evidence from interested cultural informants, like East Asian capitalist men or South or West Asian fundamentalists.

Again, I am not advocating the politicization of the discipline. I am advocating a depoliticization of the politics of hostility toward a politics of friendship to come, and thinking of the role of Comparative Literature in such a responsible effort.

If we seek to supplement gender training and human rights intervention by expanding the scope of Comparative Literature, the proper study of literature may give us entry to the performativity of cultures as instantiated in narrative. Here we stand outside, but not as anthropologist; we stand rather as reader with imagination ready for the effort of othering, however imperfectly, as an end in itself. It is a peculiar end, for "It cannot be motivated . . . except in the requirement for an increase or a supplement of justice [here to the text], and so in the experience of an inadequation or an incalculable disproportion."[18] This is preparation for a patient and provisional and forever deferred arrival into the performative of the other, in order not to transcode but to draw a response. Believe me, there is a world of difference between the two positions. In order to reclaim the role of teaching literature as training the imagination—the great inbuilt instrument of othering—we may, if we work as hard as old-fashioned Comp. Lit. is known to be capable of doing, come close to the irreducible work of translation, not from language to language but from body to ethical semiosis, that incessant shuttle that is a "life."

This last sentence draws on the work of Melanie Klein, which I have elsewhere summarized as follows:[19]

The human infant grabs on to some one thing and then things. This grabbing (*begreifen* as in *das Begriff* or concept) of an outside indistinguishable from an inside constitutes an inside, going back and forth and coding everything into a sign-system by the thing(s) grasped. One can call this crude coding a "translation." In this never-ending shuttle, violence translates into conscience and vice versa. From birth to death this "natural" machine, programming the mind perhaps as genetic instructions program the body (where does body stop and mind begin?) is partly metapsychological and therefore outside the grasp of the mind. Thus "nature" passes and repasses into "culture," in a work or shuttling site of violence (deprivation—evil—shocks the infant system-in-the-making more than satisfaction— some say *Paradiso* is the dullest of *The Divine Comedy*— but the passage from mind to body is also violent as such): the violent production of the precarious subject of reparation and responsibility. To plot this weave, the reader—in my estimation, Klein was more a reader than an analyst in the strict Freudian sense—, translating the incessant translating shuttle into that which is read, must have the most intimate access to the rules of representation and permissible narratives which make up the substance of a culture, and must also become responsible and accountable to the writing/translating of the presupposed original.[20]

It is in this painstaking supplementation of the impatient bounty of human rights that we encounter the limit of that moving frontier of Area Studies/Comparative Literature that is always a "discipline to come," through a type of language learning that fosters access to textuality. Part of this uncertain future is the growing virtualization of frontiers. What we are witnessing in the postcolonial and globalizing world is a return of the demographic, rather than territorial, frontiers that pre-date and are larger than capitalism. These demographic frontiers, responding to large-scale migration, are now appropriating the contemporary version of virtual reality and creating the kind of parastate collectivities that belonged to the shifting multicultural empires that preceded monopoly capitalism. The problem with the Bernheimer report was that it responded only to the unexamined culturalism of such symptomatic collectivities, the stereotyped producers and consumers of Cultural/Ethnic Studies.

But these are matters for the next two chapters. For now I want to repeat my concern for the literary specificity of the autochthone, which, lost in the shuffle between Cultural Studies and Comparative Literature, could not appear at all in *Comparative Literature in the Age of Multiculturalism*. Comparative Literature and Area Studies *can* work together in the fostering not only of national literatures of the global South but also of the writing of countless indigenous languages in the world that were programmed to vanish when the maps were made. The literatures in English produced by the former British colonies in Africa and Asia should be studied and supported. And who can deny the Spanish and Portuguese literatures of Latin America? Yet the languages that were historically prevented from having a constituted readership or are now losing readership might be allowed to prosper as well, even as the writers contribute to our need for languages. We do not need to map them. Together we can offer them the solidarity of borders that are easily crossed, again and again, as a permanent from-below interruption of a Comparative Literature to come, the irony of globalization.[21]

As far as I am concerned, then, there is nothing necessarily new about the new Comparative Literature. Nonetheless, I must acknowledge that the times determine how the necessary vision of "comparativity" will play out. Comparative Literature must always cross borders. And crossing borders, as Derrida never ceases reminding us via Kant, is a problematic affair.[22]

I have remarked above that borders are easily crossed from metropolitan countries, whereas attempts to enter from the so-called peripheral countries encounter bureaucratic and policed frontiers, altogether more difficult to penetrate. In spite of the fact that the effects of globalization can be felt all over the world, that there are satellite dishes in Nepalese villages, the opposite is never true. The everyday cultural detail, condition and effect of sedimented cultural idiom, does not come up into satellite country. Putting it this way should make it immediately obvious that the solution is not clear-cut. Let us postpone solution talk and consider a staging of such restricted permeability in Maryse Condé's first novel.

An important infrastructural problem of the restricted permeability of global culture is the lack of communication within and among the immense heterogeneity of the subaltern cultures of the world. In Maryse Condé's *Heremakhonon*, there is a moment when an undisclosed West African subaltern speaker, possibly feminine, says to the French-speaking upper-class young woman from Guadaloupe, who will later compliment herself on knowing Creole, "What strangeness that country [*quelle étrangeté ce pays*] which produced [*qui ne produisait*] neither Mandingo, nor Fulani, nor Toucouleur, nor Serer, nor Woloff, nor Toma, nor Guerze, nor Fang, nor Fon, nor Bété, nor Ewe, nor Dagbani, nor Yoruba, nor Mina, nor Ibo. And it was still Blacks who lived there [*Et c'étaient tout de même des Noirs qui vivaient là*!]."[23] The young woman passes this by, noting only her pleasure at being complimented on her appearance: " 'Are all the women of that country as pretty as Mademoiselle?' I got a silly pleasure out of hearing this." Is this characterization or political comment? How far should literature be read as sociological evidence? We should at least note that Condé herself remarks, in the preface to the much later second French edition, "I had the idea of putting the narrative in the mouth of a negative heroine."[24] Where on this grid of reading literature as text and/or evidence of uneven permeability shall we put a graduate student's comment that the subaltern's remark is improbable, because only an academically educated person would know such a comprehensive list of African languages? The least sense of the shifting demographics of Africa would correct this.

Commenting after the fact on the lines of communication among countries colonized by the same power in the previous centuries, it is possible to speak of an "enabling violation." Perhaps these languages died, but they got French.[25] Can one make such an uninvolved judgment about changes happening in one's own time?

In Richard Philcox's brilliant translation of the passage from Condé I have cited above we read "Fulani and Toucouleur" for the French "Peul and Toucouleur" in the list of languages. Let us pause a moment on this detail of translation, which the metropolitan reader of the translation will undoubtedly pass over.

The Fulbe are a distinct people who apparently originated [text for unpacking there] just above the Sahel between Mauritania and Mali and over the centuries migrated through the savannah of West Africa as far as the Lake Chad area. One of the areas they settled was the mid-Senegal valley. The mid-valley people referred to themselves as Haalpulaar'en (singular Haalpulaar, speaker of pulaar), whether they were pastoralists or cultivators. It was the nineteenth century French ethnographers who divided these people into distinct groups: the largely non-Muslim pastoralists were called peuls while the mostly Muslim agriculturalists were called toucouleurs. English travelers to the Sokoto Palisades (in present day Nigeria) adopted the Hausa word for the Fulbe there—Fulani.[26]

These proper names of languages carry the sedimentation of the history of the movement of peoples. Strictly speaking, Fulani includes both Peul and Toucouleur, and so is not an appropriate alternative for the latter. But the implied reader of the translation is not expected to have this information. The idea of shifting demographic frontiers caught in the virtuality of the Internet and telecommunication is generally assigned to postmodern globalization. The best among the globalizers know that there may be a history here. The eminent globality theorist, Professor Saskia Sassen, for example, invokes shifting demographic frontiers and admits that she needs a historical fix.[27] I had quoted this passage from Condé in answer when she expressed that need, but could not complete the reading. Today, in this more appropriate context, I finish the task.

The new Comparative Literature makes visible the import of the translator's choice. In the translation from *French* to *English* lies the disappeared history of distinctions in another space—made by the French and withdrawn by the English—full of the movement of languages and peoples still in historical sedimentation at the bottom, waiting for the real virtuality of our imagination. If we remain confined to English language U.S. Cultural Studies, we will not be instructed either by the staging of restricted permeability or by the disappeared text of the translation from and into the European national languages that form the basis of what we know as Comparative Literature. Cultural Studies, tied to plot summary masquerading as analysis of representation, and character analysis by a precritical model of motivation or an unearned psychoanalytic vocabulary would reduce *Heremakhonon* to a *Bildungsroman* about Veronica. The old country—an undifferentiated "Africa"—exists as a backdrop for the New World African. And for Comparative Literature it does not exist at all.

I return, then, to my general argument in this opening chapter: collaborate with and transform Area Studies. A reading of *Heremakhonon* would, for example, be strengthened by a sense of Africa that might emerge from such collaboration, for the text stages the folly of imagining an undifferentiated "Africa" as a backdrop for the New World African.

There are, of course, many institutional obstacles to such collaboration. Among them is institutional fear on both sides. Disciplinary fear. The social sciences fear the radical impulse in literary studies, and over the decades, we in the humanities have trivialized the social sciences into their rational expectation straitjackets, not recognizing that, whatever the state of the social sciences in our own institution, strong tendencies toward acknowledging the silent but central role of the humanities in the area studies paradigm are now around. Sustained and focused discussion is all the more necessary as the boundaries of disciplinary knowledge are being redrawn.

If the distaste for the social sciences and Area Studies can be overcome, there is, as we have already seen, the fear of Cultural Studies. We are afraid to let the permeability be unrestricted by our own moves. Suppose through the approved channel of Francophony, Teutophony, Lusophony, Anglophony, Hispanophony, they should begin to want to "rediscover their 'heritage' languages and cultures?"[28] Since, in this scenario, Area Studies are odious, we will be back in Cultural Studies, monolingual, presentist, narcissistic, not practiced enough in close reading even to understand that the mother tongue is actively divided.

In such a scenario it is hard not to read literature, sometimes, as a didactic aid. Let me invite you to compare the fear of Cultural Studies to this picture painted by the Magistrate, a benevolent imperialist, for the fearful young imperialist officer in J. M. Coetzee's *Waiting for the Barbarians*:

> [The barbarians] do not doubt that one of these days we [the colonizers] will pack our carts and depart to wherever it was we came from, that our buildings will become homes for mice and lizards, that their beasts will graze on these rich fields we have planted. You smile? Shall I tell you something? Every year the lakewater grows a little more salty. There is a simple explanation—never mind what it is. The barbarians know this fact. At this very moment they are saying to themselves, "Be patient, one of these days their crops will start withering from the salt, they will not be able to feed themselves, they will go." That is what they are thinking. That they will outlast us.[29]

Throughout this chapter, I have, in a rather utopian manner, been repeatedly urging a joining of forces between Comparative Literature and Area Studies, because the times seem to have come up to meet me halfway. I have confessed that I am aware of the strong forces at work against the possibility of such a coalition. At first glance, I have suggested that it is disciplinary fear that seems to keep out Area Studies. But there is also the fear, I have added, that at this point, the "new" Area

Studies might lead us back to the fear of the loss of quality control seething under the surface of the original Bernheimer report. The ominous humor of Mary Louise Pratt's invocation of George Orwell's *Animal Farm* reflects that general unease:

> Let us imagine . . . that we CompLit types are the animals in the coops and pens. The farmer no longer exists. He has retired to Florida, and before he left, he opened all the doors and gates. What do we want to do? The foxes now have access to the henhouse; the hens, however, are free to go somewhere else. Animals will move from pasture to pasture and pen to pen; strange matings will occur and new creatures [be] born. The manure pile will be invaded and its winter warmth enjoyed by all. It will be a while till new order and new leadership emerge. But the farmer won't be back.[30]

In fact, the farmer did not go far. Today the backlash is on the rise. There is a demand for humanism, with a nod toward Asia; for universalism, however ambiguous; for quality control; to fight terrorism.

For a way out, in the new Comparative Literature, I turn again to Coetzee's novel. *Waiting for the Barbarians* is, perhaps like all qualitative rather than quantitative texts, also a staging of what may be called logic and rhetoric—assuming that they can be so neatly distinguished. There are passages that resemble the one I have quoted above, where the protocol may be called "logical" when placed in distinction from what I am going to call "rhetorical." These logical passages are often accounts of the fruits of imperial experience, as above, with some historical generalizability within the loose outlines of the narrative. Over against these are the many passages where the Magistrate tries to grasp the barbarian in an embrace that is both singular and responsible. The exemplary singularity is "the girl," a young barbarian woman whose name we never learn, whose name perhaps neither the Magistrate nor the writer figure knows. The staging of rhetoricity in the novel is the Magistrate's attempt to decipher her. This is quite different from the staging of the logical Magistrate, a capable and experienced senior official who is able to summarize the characteristics of empire. A series of dreams may be one account of this deciphering effort. To have sex with the girl is another.

The Magistrate, usually a promiscuous man, is generally unable to perform what would be recognizable as an act of sex with this young barbarian woman. What comes through in his efforts to do so is his repeated generalization that the meaning of his own acts is not clear if he tries to imagine her perspective: "I feed her, shelter her, use her body, if that is what I am doing, in this foreign way."[31] I cannot forget that Freud urges us to investigate the uncanny because we are ourselves *Fremdsprächig*, "foreign speakers."[32] What can it mean but seeing the other as placed, native?

The girl is returned to her people. In a surprising example of characterological asyndeton or *recusatio*, the Magistrate intervenes on behalf of tortured barbarian prisoners and is himself tortured brutally and systematically. His imprisonment, which comes before this, reduces him to nothing. Coetzee describes him describing his deciphering effort thus: "So I continue to swoop and circle around the irreducible figure of the girl, casting one net of meaning after another over her. . . . What does she see? The protecting wings of a guardian albatross or the black shape of a coward crow afraid to strike while its prey yet breathes?"

The passage begins with a paradox. The logic of noncontradiction requires that what is irreducible is truth, not figure. The passage continues with a figuring of the undecidability of meaning. Web after web is thrown. But the meaning that is sought is the meaning of the Magistrate as subject, as perceived by the barbarian as other. This meaning is undecidable in at least two ways. First, there is no stable declaration of meaning. And second, the alternative possibilities of the meaning of the dominant self in the eyes of the barbarian other are given as questions. It is possible to suggest that two alternatives are standing in for an indefinite structure of possibilities here.

Of course, the literary is not a blueprint to be followed in unmediated social action. But if as teachers of literature we teach reading, literature can be our teacher as well as our object of investigation. And, since we are imprisoned in the vicious circle of our stakes in institutional power, the Magistrate's researches in extremis can perhaps rearrange our desires. With team teaching and institutional goodwill, we can continue to supplement Area Studies with this lesson in view. Our own undecidable meaning is in the irreducible figure that stands in for the eyes of the other. This is the effortful task: to displace the fear of our faceless students, behind whom are the eyes of the global others.

Otherwise, who crawls into the place of the "human" of "humanism" at the end of the day, even in the name of diversity? We must consider "Collectivities."

CHAPTER 2

COLLECTIVITIES

We are going to redo Comparative Literature, then, looking for our definition in the eyes of the other, as figured in the
text. Easier said than done, for literature is not a blueprint for
action. The question "Who are we?" is part of the pedagogic
exercise. In the previous chapter, I spoke of the disciplinary
fear that seems to me to permeate Comparative Literature at
the crossroads. Insofar as Comparative Literature remains part
of the Euro–U.S. cultural dominant, it shares another sort of
fear, the fear of undecidability in the subject of humanism.[1]

Who slips into the place of the "human" of "humanism" at the end of the day?

As we saw in the last chapter, liberal multiculturalism has been on the agenda of Comparative Literature for some time. Cultural Studies and Ethnic Studies are on the rise, and many minority protests that I have witnessed say, in effect, "Do not racially profile us, we are Americans." When we take such protests into the academic arena, we see outlines of an already existing multiculturalist Comparative Literature, Area Studies already urged to cross borders by *Crossing Borders*. My question—Who are "we"?—is now more complicated. If we are serious about advanced instruction in Comparative Literature, we have to ask the question of the formation of collectivities without necessarily prefabricated contents.

Real answers come in the classroom and are specific to that changeful site. In this chapter I merely read some texts that stage the question of collectivity. I have chosen difficult, even mysterious texts, for the question is often too easily answered in the heat of identity politics, in the classroom, in the media, in electoral politics, in war and peace, everywhere. If I give way to that ease, I will not have moved you a step. Bear with me as I read these curious texts, where collectivities become undecidable—a sort of comparativist sampler: Derrida and Woolf, Tayeb Salih, Mahasweta Devi. There may be a pattern here: an internal undecidability within "European" texts (Derrida is sometimes European); undecidability between Europe and its other, in sexual difference; and undecidability between the human and its other. These are warning texts, perhaps. In committee, we must proceed with certainties. When we seem to have won or lost in terms of certainties, we must, as literature teachers in the classroom, remember such warnings—let literature teach us that there are no certainties, that the process is open, and that it may be altogether salutary that it is so. I will do my best to explain, but I am hampered by the fact that I am not out to demystify.

In order to assume culture we must assume collectivity. Yet usually we assume collectivity on the basis of culture. This move can be called by many names. European classical rhetoric will give you *hysteron proteron*, which the *American Heritage Dictionary* defines as "the logical fallacy of . . . using as a premise a proposition that is yet to be proved." You can call it a variety of metalepsis, the substitution of effect for cause. You can call it a ruse that bases the constative on a performative that requires the constative in order to be felicitous. I will call it begging the question, assuming culture at the origin begs the question of collectivity. And the collectivity that is presumed to be the condition and effect of humanism is the human family itself.

In his labyrinthine and painstaking reading of Carl Schmitt in *Politics of Friendship*, Jacques Derrida circles around surprisingly "common sense" points about the formation of collectivities.[2] In my estimation, that book is an example of how the humanities and the social sciences must supplement each other. That is also my general point in this book, upstream from Comparative Literature and Area Studies. I will summarize a few of Derrida's points: democracy is a public system, but friendship is also private; thoughts of democracy entail brotherhood, and that may become violently exclusivist; collectivities are undeterminable; decisions are always taken too soon and in the dark; including women as women would lead to unpredictable consequences. This last part will bring us to Virginia Woolf and Gertrude Stein.

Derrida embeds his reading of Schmitt in a consideration of the many politics of thinking friendship—thinking the friend, thinking friends, enterprises that are by no means identical. There can be no politics without collectivity. Derrida begins his book by offering the practical difficulties of forming a collectivity without a group that at least presents itself as a collectivity of friends. It is not possible to think a collectivity of enemies. "Are friends rare?" "What is friendship? How or what is it? What is a friend?" (PF 8).

The confrontation of old Comparative Literature and Cultural/Ethnic Studies can be polarized into humanism versus identity politics.[3] Both sides trivialize reading and writing as the allegory of knowing and doing. Both serve as powerful performative examples of an unexamined politics of collectivity. I read the beginning of *Politics of Friendship* as a reminder that in order to confront this we must engage the classroom (even when it has no walls, I must add). Derrida tells us that the book is no more than "the first session of a seminar conducted with th[e] title, 'Politics of Friendship,' in 1988–89. . . . Week after week . . . each session . . . tried . . . to see if the scenography could be set in motion around itself. This text . . . *represents*, only the first session . . . less a first act than a sort of preview" (PF vii–viii; translation modified). *Politics of Friendship* is, in other words, only a book between covers. For the real text, you must enter the classroom, put yourself to school, *as* a preview of the formation of collectivities. A single "teacher's" "students," flung out into the world and time, is, incidentally, a real-world example of the precarious continuity of a Marxism "to come," aligned with grassroots counterglobalizing activism in the global South today, with little resemblance to those varieties of "Little Britain" leftism that can take on board the binary opposition of identity politics and humanism, shifting gears as the occasion requires.

The fragility of collectivity enters a discussion of the originary curvature that is the law of the social as such. Derrida writes, to the reader as well as to those absent students:

How are we to distinguish between ourselves, between each of us who compose this as yet so undetermined "we"? Let us therefore suppose that you already held [*teniez déjà*] me responsible for what I say, by the simple fact that I am speaking, even if I am not yet assuming responsibility for the sentences that I am quoting. Then, perhaps, you will grant me this, as the first result of a practical demonstration, that which has just taken place: even before the question of responsibility was posed to us, of "speaking in one's own name," countersigning such and such an affirmation, etc., we are caught, the ones and the others, in a sort of heteronomic and dissymetrical curvature of social space, more precisely of the relationship with the other: before all organized *socius*, before all *politeia*, before all determined "government," *before* all "law." Prior to and before it, in the sense of Kafka's "before the law." (PF 230)

We must learn not to dismiss such gestures as rhetorical extravagances. To buttress the earlier notion of the future anterior, where one promises no future present but attends upon what will have happened as a result of one's work, Derrida now adds a new kind of "perhaps," "the possibilization of [an] impossible possible [that] must remain at one and the same time as undecidable—and therefore as decisive—as the future itself" (PF 29). Given the irreducible curvature of social space—the heteronomic curvature of the relationship with the other—the political must act in view of such a "perhaps." Because we cannot decide it, it remains decisive, the unrestricted gamble of all claims to collectivity, agonistic or otherwise. Derrida knows the interminable indeterminacy of epistemic change in the agent, not only through his theoretical elaborations but also, as his specific invocation of the classroom at the beginning of *Politics of Friendship* indicates, as a teacher in the humanities. It is in that class that the question "How many are we?" is asked.

The law of curvature—that one cannot access another directly and with a guarantee (by "appresentational analogy" only, Husserl will write)—is not a deterrent to politics.[4] By suggesting that the philosophical position of being called by the other be accessed by its inscription into political responsibility, Derrida demands a more risky political activity. (In the context of this book, a disciplinary politics of distant reading and the scopic ambitions of mapping the world's literatures and bringing it under Euro–U.S. rational control would be questioned by that suggestion.) In one of the first invocations of Nietzsche in the book, Derrida describes a Nietzschean model of friendship in "analogical apresentation": "solitary . . . but . . . all[ied] . . . in silence within the necessity of keeping silent together" (PF 54–55). If you call this imperative to straighten the curve (the impossibility of straightforward access, the possibility of good turning into evil)—*courbure* into *droiture*—a "madness," it is a madness that writes the history of politics. Any political philosophy that does not take this grounding errancy into account will cover over the impossibility of simple collectivities with various ruses.[5]

Derrida points out that both friendship and enmity are internally contradictory, and political decisionism must negotiate with the undecidable. The difference between "left" and "right" begins after this structurally shared "madness" of the political. For now, I take up a few pedagogic hints from Derrida's text where they resonate with my own.

Derrida considers the implications of the performative contradiction in Aristotle's apostrophe "O my friends, there is no friend," and the consequences of the folded-over constative version: "he who has too many friends has none" (PF 209; translation modified). "We must approach these differences wherever they count: in the modality of uttering, in the meaning of the sentence, in the chain of philosophemes, in the very politics that bends or operates there" (PF 217). Are you calling to arms or stating a science? Vocative or nominative? Or do the two get messed up inevitably? Common sense, practical politics.

Derrida brings the rich notion of *teleopoiesis*—teleopoietic rather than legitimizing reversal—into play many times in his book. That is indeed one of the shocks to the idea of belonging, to affect the distant in a *poiesis*—an imaginative making—without guarantees, and thus, by definitive predication, reverse its value. Again, note the difference between this and the mechanical convenience of mapmaking. "The teleopoiesis we are speaking of is a messianic structure. . . . We are not yet among these philosophers of the future, we who are calling them and calling them the philosophers of the future, but we are in advance their friends. . . . This is perhaps the 'community of those without community'" (PF 37; see also PF 172). (Transforming the philosopheme into a disciplinary allegory, I ask us to imagine ourselves outside the top-heavy German/Romance Comparative Literature, scrabbling for control, rationalizing sanctioned ignorance, pointing at European intellectual enclaves already present in earlier colonial formations as "history," toward those readers of the future.) It is with careful accounting for time lags that effective collectivities are formed. Therefore Derrida asks: Who is the contemporary? (PF 77).

Active teleopoiesis in all moments of decision makes the task of reading imperative and yet indecisive. In closing this chapter I will look at two teleopoietic displacements of *Heart of Darkness*—in Arabic and in Bengali. In our everyday, the broadest institutional collectivity imaginable is democracy. It is useful for us that *Politics of Friendship* asks: Can democracy—invariably claimed as a politics, or perhaps *the* politics of friendship—function without a logofratrocentric notion of collectivity? With the sister allowed in rarely, and only as an honorary brother (PF 201)? Let us step back.

Virginia Woolf's *A Room of One's Own* took a step toward answering this question. I want to get to that enhancement, of "perhaps" and paradox, at an angle, by first looking at how Woolf prefigures one of Derrida's concerns as I have summarized them: the unpredictable consequences of inserting women as women into the question of friendship. I cannot promise that this will lead to unmediated institutional consequences for our disciplines as they stand. But if in the last chapter I exhorted you to think of the ungraspable other as the figured origin of our definitions, today I emphasize the unimaginable future "to come." It is in that spirit that I point at an unpredictable filiation—unfortunate word caught in the very history we are unraveling—between Woolf and groups I have learned to touch, perhaps, in the last ten years. For Virginia Woolf, one of the greatest gains brought by the emancipation of women was the possibility of writing, in fiction: "Chloe liked Olivia. . . . For if Chloe liked Olivia and Mary Carmichael knows how to express it she will light a torch in that vast chamber where nobody has yet been. . . . And I began to read the book again, and read how Chloe watched Olivia put a jar on a shelf and say how it was time to go home to her children."[6]

In my fleeting but regular and intimate contact with subaltern cultural formations, I have come to intuit an originary queerness within which the heterosexual bond is loosely contained as a social focus of loyalty and parenting. Indeed, U.S. idiom, which names *same*-sex "queer," has an unwitting descriptive—though not necessarily axiological—hierarchy that would be irrelevant to these cultural formations.[7] That the development of the nuclear family has something like a relationship with the self-determination of capital is by now an old story.[8] I myself have been making the argument for some time now that on the ethical register, *pre*capitalist cultural formations should not be regarded in an evolutionist way, with capital as the telos.[9] Culturally inscribed dominant mindsets that are defective for capitalism should rather be nurtured for grafting onto our dominant so that we can learn from them ways to assure that they do not forever remain outside the lines of mobility. This is a task for which all preparation can only be indirect. That style of work, which I will touch upon in the next chapter, does not affect university education in its detail and therefore is not part of this book. It does, however, operate as a baseline critique of the social Darwinism implicit in all our ideas of "development" in the economic sense, "hospitality" in the narrow sense, and scopic Eurocentric Comparative Literature as an alternative. It taps what Walter Benjamin calls, in a lovely aside, "the educative power, which in its perfected form, stands outside the law."[10]

I bring this up here because Woolf's intuitions of a general queerness within which reproductive sexuality can find its limited socialization (Chloe likes Olivia but goes home to her children) is an open-ended structure that can be reconstellated, levered off from its textual location, copied from Bloomsbury and pasted onto the narrative I put together above. Woolf herself does not name it (some species of) "queer," inscribed hierarchically within the history of the language in relationship to "straight." She does not simply reverse its value and thus legitimize the hierarchy. The way she writes, we are free to copy and paste, as we do even when we are reading the most restrictive text. Indeed, if we want to see this specific binary opposition abyssalized in the transformation of democracy from "Enlightenment" to postcolony, we go to J. M. Coetzee's *Disgrace*.[11] That novel offers a glimpse of what happens when the woman is no longer an honorary brother, a figuration of the impossible. The moment in *A Room of One's Own* serves as a model for reconstellating, copying and pasting for editing, teleopoiesis. It seems to inhabit the same structure—heteronormativity contained within the "queer"—that I intuit in the precapitalist formation for which I have been working. For Woolf the structure heralds a new gendered collectivity—a gendered notion of friendship.

Copying (rather than cutting) and pasting—teleopoiesis—is part of the general technique of the new comparative literature, and I am grateful to Jacques Derrida for the word, which allows us to suspect that all poiesis may be a species of teleopoiesis, although we might keep the difference intact—as the difference between event and task, provisionally, practically. The most important thing, as far as I can tell, is knowing how to let go. And here fiction, as I suggested in the previous chapter, can be a teacher. If you push literary criticism to its logical end it becomes either absolute creative freedom (slyly supported by some corporate entity, as in the case of the Saatchi brothers in Britain) or maximum verifiability (as in the case of legalistic "demonstrate by textual reference" literary criticism).[12] We must learn to let go, remember that it is the singular unverifiability of the literary from which we are attempting to discern collectivities. Let us consider Virginia Woolf letting go, at the end of *A Room of One's Own*.

As she is winding down her famous exhortation to young Oxbridge women, she says to her listeners, "you should embark upon another stage of your . . . career. A thousand pens are ready to suggest what you should do and what effect you will have. My own suggestion is a little fantastic, I admit; I prefer, therefore, to put it in the form of fiction" (RO 113).

She inaugurates a ghost dance, asking all aspiring woman writers in England to be haunted by the ghost of Shakespeare's sister. She quite gives up the "room of one's own and £500 a year" in her closing words: "I maintain that she would come if we worked for her, and that so to work, *even in poverty and obscurity*, is worth while" (RO 114; emphasis mine).

What does it mean "to work for her," especially as a principle for the formation of an unintended collectivity? The only semirestrictive clue offered by Woolf, "even in poverty," makes it clear that the work is not necessarily connected to the economic dominant giving aid. Apart from that, and in my estimation, the lack of specificity there, as encompassing as a shifter that anyone can inhabit, is as powerful as it is dangerous. We have to work at that word "work," elaborate it. Let me now try, in the name of a new Comparative Literature, to lead us out of a restricted disciplinary circuit. It is perhaps what was always written in my untimely sense of the inclusiveness of Comparative Literature. For now, I will call this work open-plan fieldwork.

I am using this phrase to point at two kinds of work outside salaried work, in which I have been engaged for a little over ten years and at which I already hinted above: one is to associate with constructive counterglobalizing networks of people's alliances in what is now called the global South, for want of a better term; the other is the one-on-one effort to establish barefoot schools and to train local teachers of children in two aboriginal pockets in western West Bengal. Strange as it may sound, this second one is the longest possible-term preparation for the supplementation of something like the social sciences by the humanities. I am not going to explain this any further now. This second kind of work is much harder to talk about and I have tried to do so at great length elsewhere.[13] This is now my own real training ground: learning to learn from below to devise a practical philosophy to train members of the largest sector of the future electorate and to train its current teachers in the habits of democratic reflexes (before one necessarily engages the understanding of specific content) and on a one-on-one basis; not to give in to the innumerable so-called nonformal education projects without patient commitment to linguistic and ethical othering in the trainer; to abhor nationalist idealism and identitarianism: efforts to produce collectivities in classrooms, not unrelated to Derrida; "working for them," not unrelated to Woolf; a Europeanist comparativist education used from below—"ab-used," as I have said elsewhere.[14] I am convinced that in such areas, this is an impulse that is necessary, though perhaps, in the last analysis, impossible.[15] However remote the possibility, this too can be an itinerary of the new comparative literature.

I want to be able to keep this as a point of reference while I show how much I am interested, because it is part of the same big picture, in tertiary education in the United States. Perhaps the gap between Manbhum (one of the areas where I run schools) and Manhattan is unbridgeable. An aporia. But to want to cross aporias differently is one way of thinking choice, surely? Surely I am obliged to rewrite the aporia as a moral dilemma: How is it possible to reconcile what I touch in the field—other people—with what I teach for a living—literary criticism? Here is crossing borders, another way.

Open-plan fieldwork, then. Sketchy words, imprecise description. It is silly simply to exhort U.S. students—especially self-consciously hyphenated ones— to get into this new kind of mindset with no institutional backup and no precise description, in order to revise a descriptive of collectivities elsewhere. "Fieldwork" belongs to the social sciences. As far as I know, disciplinary critique in the social sciences has been in *how* you write up fieldwork, given who you are—in critical anthropology, in radical qualitative sociology, in oral or narrative history. At any rate, the idea of fieldwork where you do not transform your field experience into a Euro–U.S. model academic code of some kind, however relaxed, is an idea I got from my so-called activist experience, where I am an amateur. How can I expect institutionally trained social scientists to take any interest?

As I was going through such self-questioning, I heard a job talk by a young African American sociologist on the subject of hate crimes. One of her observations, stated without obvious irony, has remained in my mind: "the police were clear on the question of intent, the lawyers were unclear, and the activists were confused." She believed she should transcode this problem into a dissertation. I think I can understand the impatience of the serious social science academic in the face of the impassioned activist without deep background, but still I was dismayed. When I questioned her, she agreed with me that, in the social field, in the interest of the rule of law, we need clarity. The social science dissertation writer was therefore helping the lawyers, distinguishing them from activists, so that only the enforcers of the law should not be clear-headed, following orders. On the other hand, it seemed to me that it was the "confused activist" type that came closest to the (less "professionalized" or apathetic) humanities student—not in the juridico-legal calculus, yet concerned with social justice: Cultural Studies/Ethnic Studies.

Now my moral dilemma began to take a more institutional shape: How can I, as a reader of literature, supplement the social sciences? This attached itself to my initial anxiety for the infilitration of Area Studies. Aristotle could get away with saying that imaginative making—*poiesis*—is a better instrument of knowledge—*philosophoteron*—than *istoria*, but I cannot, especially since we live in a time and a place that has privatized the imagination and pitted it against the political. Begin to see that all poiesis is teleopoiesis, I say above. Think that eventuality as a task, even as a persistent institutional task "to come."

I found an analogy in the situation of the international group called "Doctors Without Frontiers," whose members travel to solve health problems and dispense healing all over the world.[16] They cannot be involved in the repetitive work of primary health care, which requires changes in the habit of what seems normal living. Doctors Without Frontiers cannot learn all the local languages, dialects, and idioms of the places where they provide help. They use local interpreters. As the benevolent triumphalism of today's transnationality crosses borders at ease, open-plan fieldwork calls for the role of the interpreter. Hegemonic Comparative Literature would continue the analogy: use local interpreters. To displace this institutionally, let us cultivate, rather, the role of the interpreter: inter-diction—speaking between the two sides—as persistent calculus. How does this relate to the question of woman in democracy, which allowed me the transition from Derrida to Woolf?

When Doctors Without Frontiers began their work there was no pervasive and global NGO culture. Today, with the highly gendered and self-styled International Civil Society—the positive name for that which is *not* the state (*nongovernmental*)—it can perhaps be advanced that inserting women into the question of institutionalized friendship ("democracy"—as the code name for the political restructuring entailed by the transformation of [efficient through inefficient to wild] state capitalisms and their colonies to tributary economies of rationalized global financialization) is leading to consequences seemingly as predictable as electronic databasing can make them: impatient philanthropy caught in organizational priorities rather than continuing hands-on engagements that would allow nonhierarchical understanding to develop; intervention into cultural systems in the mere name of "woman." The

United Nations in its contemporary formation operates as and gives shelter to the International Civil Society—the forum of NGOs.

How can an amateur activist and a longstanding student of Comparative Literature like myself supplement not only the social sciences but also benevolent social engineering by women for women? How is it possible to use what I teach for a living, literary criticism, to expand my institutional responsibility with what I learn in the field, other women—the other girl-child: Shakespeare's sister; Gramsci's women; Nagarjuna's sister; Sitting Bull's sister; Xanthippe; the sister of the Dogon Sage of Mali? How can literary studies prepare us for multiple-issue gender justice? Single issues are for office convenience.

Doctors Without Frontiers cannot enter the mysterious thicket of the languages, dialects, and idioms of the many places where members travel to help. Primary health care groups, on the other hand, if they are to remain uncoercive, must learn or be at home in the cultural idiom of the place. Otherwise the change does not stick. At this point I am clearly displacing the analogy further, wishing to add to the role of the interpreter the role of the member of the primary health care group, at home in the idiom of the culture, patiently engaging in uncoercive change in the habit of normality. This looks forward and outward to the discipline of Comparative Literature outside the Euro–U.S., flourishing, one hopes, in the many linguistic traditions because we, in our turn, are opening up toward those languages rather than reining them in. This is the possibility that is undermined by U.S.-style world literature becoming the staple of Comparative Literature in the global South.

A Room of One's Own consists of two lectures on the subject of women and fiction given at Cambridge women's colleges in

1928 and published in 1929. As I have already suggested, it turns out to be an essay on women's collectivities of various sorts.

After a few remarks about the impossibility of offering a lecture about the true nature of women and the true nature of fiction, Woolf puts her own words in the most robust mode of fiction, the age-old performative contradiction or paradox: I am a liar. She gives the paradox another spin and puts it in the passive voice: "Lies will flow from my lips," she writes. " 'I' is only a convenient term for somebody who has no real being," Woolf writes in this most persuasive text. "Lies will flow from my lips, but there may *perhaps* be some truth mixed up with them; it is for you to seek out this truth and to *decide* whether any part of it is worth keeping" (RO 4–5; emphasis mine). Let us make Woolf's "perhaps" and "decide" be infected and affected by what we have just read in Derrida.

Chapter 2 starts with the nameless "I," but in a few pages she is indirectly given the name Mary Beton. "Five hundred pounds a year for ever were left me by an aunt, Mary Beton, for no other reason than that I share her name" (RO 37). "I share her name." One is two-d; standing in for the indefinite? Remember, every use of the major shifter "I" in this text is marked. At any rate, Mary Beton now acknowledges the compromised foundations of her liberation. She owes her £500 to imperialism. Her eponymous aunt "died by a fall from her horse when she was riding out to take the air in Bombay," and Woolf's Mary Beton—who shares her name—sees money as a better alternative to democracy (RO 37).

In the last chapter, Woolf takes us into the impossible possible of the "perhaps if," as only fiction can. Consider the framing of this famous passage. "I" as Mary Beton speaks as follows: "the very first sentence that I would write here, I said, crossing over to the writing-table and taking up the page headed Women and Fiction,"—the actual talk that the real

Virginia Woolf is presenting, in the frozen time of the single occasion—"is that it is fatal for any one who writes to think of their sex. . . . One must be woman-manly or man-womanly" (RO 104).

Most readers take this sentiment to be Woolf's message to women, and try to find ways around such a strange statement. If, however, we "read" the page in its fictive mode of paradox, we will see that this fine impartial sentence is never written. The "I" as Mary Beton moves to the writing table where the empty first page of the lecture, with nothing but the title, lies waiting. It is as if all that has gone before in the book is just a story and now the real lecture will begin. But the lecture as lecture does not begin. "I would write this sentence" is where it ends. I would if I could but I can't, in the time of the book. What follows is a series of thunderous prescriptive declaratives: "it is," "it is," "it is," "no figure of speech," "it must," "it cannot," "has to," "has to," "must," "must," "must." All this in nineteen lines. And then, miraculously, what Roman Jakobson would call "the poetic function" takes over. "The principle of equivalence [is projected] from the axis of selection into the axis of combination."[17] The text undoes its lapse—the forgetting of paradox—by a sequence of declaratives. "Freedom" and "peace"—large abstractions—help the paragraph fade into the long languorous vowels of high modernist impressionist prose: "The writer . . . must pluck the petals from a rose or watch the swans float calmly down the river. . . . I thought, hearing far off the roar of London's traffic, into that tremendous stream" (RO 105). Remember that the thought comes to her as she watches a well-dressed couple enter a taxi, in the textual association of upper-class Whitehall.

This is how the celebrated thought of androgyny ends, all in the course of a paragraph. The next sentence, beginning the short last section of the book is simply: "Here, then, Mary

Beton ceases to speak. . . . I will end now in my own person"
(RO 105). A deliberate projection of a collectivity in one
name—even a fictive name—is staged as fizzling out.

Woolf's definition—"only a convenient term for somebody
who has no real being"—holds even for "my own person." In
literature as in law, language lives in the reader, who is just as
precarious an "I," with the liberty granted by Woolf's text, by
any text, to move it along elsewhere, by a provisional surren-
der in the self's stereotype, never complete. This precarious
and temporary transfer of agency, earned through imaginative
attention, is how the habit of reading and writing as robust
allegories of knowing and doing may come to supplement, fill
a hole in as well as add to, the decision-making authority of
the social sciences. By "speaking in her own person," Woolf
solicits the risk of being read.

Woolf expects this attentive reading but has not received
it. We have forgotten how to read with care. This book is
taught forever as the call for androgyny, a private room, and
five hundred pounds.

How does the reader know that the text expects attention,
this proactive behavior that is all good reading? Here is Woolf,
in this very paragraph: "you no doubt have been . . . contra-
dicting [Mary Beton] and making whatever additions and
deductions seem good to you. That is all as it should be, for in
a question like this truth is only to be had by laying together
many varieties of error" (RO 105). The reader and writer are
multiple in constituting the unverifiable truth of the text.

In her "own person," this "I" tells these young college
women, "Do not dream of influencing other people," and
admits, with an honesty still rare in public feminist profes-
sions, "Women—but are you not sick to death of the word? I
can assure you that I am. . . . The truth is, I *often* [not always,
an incredibly important detail about political collectivities] like

women" (RO 111; emphasis mine). And then comes the end, which we have already looked at: "I maintain that she would come if we worked for her, and that so to work, *even in poverty and obscurity*, is worth while" (RO 114; emphasis mine).

Simply speaking about ghost dances and the "perhaps" of the future anterior will bring me back to the social scientist's censure: "the activist is confused," and the activist's disgust: "theory's too abstract." Let us go on to note what has often been noted, and move on. In invoking Shakespeare's sister Woolf is making a possible class argument—female genius in the less privileged classes. The thought of androgyny belongs to taxicabs and Whitehall. Shakespeare's sister is buried near a bus stop (today also a stop on the London Underground) in the outskirts, named after a public house.

Aristotle had suggested that imaginative making was a better way of knowing than the historical record because it was more general, more "catholic" with a small C than the single-mindedness of history. General, therefore more generalizable? Rather different from the Latin "universal," into which the word is translated. Some readers will engage a Heideggerian polemic regarding Latin translations of Greek words here, perhaps. My interest is humbler: simply to suggest that what is generalizable is, by that token, susceptible to cutting and pasting, poiesis trembling into the task of teleopoiesis.

If you can accompany me in my reading, something uncannily like the general structure of *A Room of One's Own* can be seen as being replayed in so-called "transnational" feminism today.[18] The former helps me know the latter, as follows.

If I, Mary Beton, self-supporting by the grace of imperialism, could, then I would write that, "other things being equal," as they say, the opening presupposition of an ideal unwritten talk should be that men and women are equal participants in the literary enterprise. Let us rewrite the last sentence, keeping the general structure intact: if I, Mary Beton, self-supporting by the grace of neocolonialism and globalization, could, then I would write the opening presupposition of all the Declarations of Women in Development and Gender and Development to say that women of the global dominant, from all the countries of the world, and women who suffer poverty everywhere could be equal. The rhetorical conduct of Woolf's text does not let the sentence become a declarative. That tiny detail, I am free because my aunt, another Mary Beton, died specifically in Bombay; a remark in the concluding section that "your chance of earning five hundred pounds a year would be minute in the extreme [but for] two wars—the Crimean and the European War" (RO 108)—what we now call World War I; and the incursion of the poetic function halt the text even as it steps forward.

We must now distinguish between two kinds of generalities. The generality of poiesis depends on its unverifiability; it cannot be tied to a singular "fact." There is another kind of generality, which must suppress singularity in order to establish a "fact." It is, if you like, the difference between prefiguration and prediction.

As long as transnational feminism operates without the caution in Woolf's text, the second type of generalization must operate there, to establish a generalized name of "woman." This is to ensure predictability in the field of women. "Woman" is the word that has been taken for granted by the UN, ever since the beginning, in Mexico City (1975), of the large-scale women's conferences. Within a certain broadly defined group of the world's women, with a certain degree of flexibility in class and politics, the assumptions of a sex-gender system, an unacknowledged biological determination of behavior, and an object-choice scenario defining female life (children and/or public life; population control and/or development) are shared at least as common currency. With this basic prep, and in the domain of gendered intervention, today's UN and the World Bank operate in the field of gender.

The modern Mary Beton would like to write that first sentence on a clean slate: that the woman denied access to upward social mobility, although outside of this commonality, can be accessed and put on the way to global-local (in the place of the male-female that the earlier Mary Beton conjured with) equality. In order to start with this first sentence as a declaration rather than a subjunctive, a whole group of Mary Betons will define not other women's ways of acting but their ways of suffering others' action, how they suffer specific kinds of victimization so that they can be given specific kinds of help. The group's most overt tabulation was the Beijing six-point Platform of Action, drafted in 1995. There was, and is, something grand in the effort to bring the world's women under one rule of law, one civil society, administered by the women of the internationally divided dominant, two collectivities seen as one.

Even as we understand the Encyclopedist grandeur of this design, we must also see that it is the exact structural replica of the grand design to bring the world's rural poor under one rule of finance, one global capital, again run by the internationally divided dominant. Our effort to change this is to attend to the fictive structure of *A Room of One's Own*, which will stretch far.

Emboldened by Woolf's text, I speak now not as the confused activist but as the literary critic who sees in imagination an instrument for giving in, without guarantees, to the teleopoietic gaze of others. In order to speak again of Shakespeare's sister, I offer a summary of the historical rather than the fictive moment of women, the dominant world structure since 1989. Globalizing capital cannot not establish the same system of exchange for all nations and thus flatten out the struggles of macro- and microeconomic history, to establish what is called "a level playing field." In more than a structural parallel, in order to establish international women's rights upon the human rights paradigm, the myriad specificities of women's histories must be flattened out to assume a history whose synchrony is something like the UN's six-point platform of action. But only something like it. There is now no other way forward, but perhaps there are constant ways of turn and return. This is not the old particularism-universalism debate. It is working with the emergence of the generalized value form, global commensurability in the field of gender, a *droiture* that must be reclaimed for the irreducibility of *courbure*, again and again. Otherwise, all the diversity of daily life escapes, inescapably. We must accept this because no movement can work without this currency now. We must even suggest that "feminism," as the minimally generalizable common element in varieties of feminist struggles, has always tended toward the emergence of the general equivalent "woman," who inhabits and must inhabit databases—as far as policy can go. Gender signals the possibility of abstraction.

We cannot and should not reject this impulse toward generalization, which has something like a relationship with globalization. If we do—and some have the ignorance and/or luxury to do so—we will throw away every good of every international initiative. The other side—the side of capital—will not (and cannot) throw away the power of the move toward the general. When today's comparative literature engages with feminism, it must keep the generalizing impulse under erasure, visible as a warning. This generality is not the textured collectivities toward which literature takes us.

In the opening paragraphs of this chapter, I reminded ourselves that work within the political or institutional calculus must operate in the realm of decidability. Yet the future is decisive only because, being unpredictable, it is not susceptible to decidability or, indeed, its opposite. The fear of undecidability is the planner's fear. I suggested that in the decisive moment, we might remember warning texts. Woolf tells the students at Oxbridge that her fantastic suggestion is made as a counter to the many decisive prescriptions for educated British women available on bookshelves in the early twentieth century.

Before the shelves filled with how-to books for women, suffrage had to be won. And democracy is the most reasonable way to assume collectivity. Let us repeat Derrida's question: Can democracy function without a logofratrocentric notion of collectivity? With the sister allowed in rarely, and only as an honorary brother? Gertrude Stein stages Susan B. Anthony (1820–1906), the suffragist leader, as answering that question in the opera on her life—*The Mother of Us All*: "having the vote [women] will become like men," the sister will become an honorary brother. In Stein's imagination of the end of the nineteenth century, it goes thus:

Susan B. . . . Men are afraid.
Anne timidly. And women.
Susan B. Ah women often have not any sense of danger, after all a hen screams pitifully when she sees an eagle but she is only afraid for her children, men are afraid for themselves. . . . Men have kind hearts when they are not afraid but they are afraid afraid afraid. . . . If I were to tell them so their kindness would turn to hate. . . .
Anne. But Susan B. you fight and you are not afraid.
Susan B. I fight and I am not afraid, I fight but I am not afraid.
Anne. And you will win.

Susan B. Win what, win what.

Anne. Win the vote for women.

Susan B. Yes some day some day the women will vote and by that time.

Anne. By that time oh wonderful time.

Susan B. By that time it will do them no good because having the vote they will become like men, they will be afraid, having the vote will make them afraid, oh I know it, but I will fight for the right, for the right to vote for them even though they become like men, become afraid like men, become like men.

([At this intolerable vision of the need to supplement rights with responsibility, and the latter gender-compromised] Anne bursts into tears. Jenny Reefer rushes in) [now all is unquestioned calculus, victory seen as victory, not warning that it is only "to come"]

Jenny Reefer. I have just converted Lillian Russell to the cause of women's suffrage. . . .[19]

Now John Adams and Daniel Webster come in and the opera gets into another gear.

Affirmative undecidability, responsibility, fruition always in the mode of "to come," for future generations, "perhaps," all this is here understood as the woman's part; rational expectations, the vote as assurance of decisiveness, is understood as the man's hope. This is how sexual difference plays in this passage. (This is text-specific, of course. The vote can also be seen as the [minimal representation] of the empty open end of what is forever "to come." And Clarice Lispector can figure precisely such a fear into a figure of collectivity: "I am a bit afraid: still a fear of letting myself go for the next instant is unknown. Is the next instant made by me? Or does it make itself all by itself? It puts us together by way of the breath.")[20]

If female friendship in *A Room of One's Own* can serve as a structure for teleopoiesis, the vote in *The Mother of Us All* can serve as a concept-metaphor of the institutional calculus recoding undecidability—as robust a contradiction as the irreducible figure as meaning (*Waiting for the Barbarians*) or the subject saying, "Lies will flow from my lips." An institutional calculus recoding or instrumentalizing undecidability may be a description of the fantastic suggestion I put forth in this book: a discipline always attempting to harness the power of fiction as it approaches Area Studies and the social science disciplines.

U.S. women did win the vote in 1920. I do not know if they became "like men," even in the sense of Stein's Anthony.

Literature cannot predict, but it may prefigure. Although the intermediate steps must perforce remain vague, the conviction that the rest of the world's women must become "like us," which I invoked in my reading of *A Room of One's Own*, is not unrelated to suffrage making us "like men"—feminism as the forgetting of sexual difference. I offer a case below, and make a connection.

In February 2000, in southern Bangladesh, I was talking to a woman from a small European country who had given up her job as a receptionist ten years earlier, to see the world, and then, since she had to look for a living, got sucked into the circuit of international women's aid. Her story is fascinating in its exemplarity. She was about to go off for a conversation with the founder of Grameen Bank. Even as I was translating at breakneck speed two local critics of the bank, it was clear that she had built the justification for microcredit on imagined Bangladeshi villages peopled by little Euro-U.S. women who happened to be Bangladeshi. Another woman, from a midwestern state, had learned not only Bengali but the regional dialect—admirable effort—but was thinking of bilingual education on the metropolitan U.S. multiculturalist model, and planning for someone from the United States to come down to teach the teachers how to think freely. Shelley wrote in 1818, referring to his contemporary British society—of labor-saving machinery, the beginning of conglomerate factories, and an explosion of knowledge and information—"We want the creative faculty to imagine that which we know."[21] These are characteristic examples of a globalized high-tech dominant feminism without frontiers that cannot imagine what it knows and does not know how to learn from below. A failure of teleopoiesis. (We saw this again as Afghan women became the flavor of the day in November 2001. "They are dating and shopping," crooned Diane Sawyer.) I cannot help but think that to deny the privilege of close reading to the texts of the global South is to give in to comparable impulses within the discipline.

This is where the mysterious imaginative undertaking of Woolf's book can still kick in; 1928 is somewhere between Shelley and the Internet. "A thousand pens are ready to suggest what you should do and what effect you will have. My own suggestion is a little fantastic." There is no mention of working to alleviate the condition of the aspiring female writer. It is simply that the women must work to make her ghost appear. "She would come if we worked for her." I call it a prayer to be haunted by her ghost, to be othered by her, unanticipatably. "So to work, even in poverty and obscurity": here, for me, is the enigmatic fictive moment that I can generalize into that inelegant and imprecise phrase "open-plan fieldwork," with unanticipatable results, if any. It is not the rich helping the poor; the workers for the ghost to appear can also work in poverty and obscurity. It is important that Woolf offers this to the female elite in the making—Oxbridge women—as an imaginative alternative. I think literary training, entering into the idiom, can patiently urge us to do this rather than always measure success by statistics or photo ops. We are a commercializing culture; we are encouraged to turn everything into money. But if we are foolish enough to take the question of collectivities seriously, we must offer this alternative to the silly cultural conservatism with which all culturally interested modifications of human rights play a dangerous game.

When I was writing the first version of this essay, I spent some time reading Luce Irigaray's *Democracy Begins Between Two*.[22] Only Europe, only male/female. We have read Derrida's *Other Heading*; there, the migrant is ungendered. Excellent attempts such as Balibar's into "Ambiguous Universality" fall short because the author must take Hegel and "the case of Western Europe" as the prime example of the normative sequence of social formations everywhere: "there is no doubt in my view that Hegel was right" that the autonomy of the private was a consequence of the triumph of the law of the state.[23] Once you are convinced of this, the next step is to take it as given that the West brought individualism to the rest of the world by pulling it into state formations; then come fresh compromises to account for every exception to this rule, circling back to the initial assumption that the rest is collectivist whereas the West is individualist. A vicious circle. I read Joan Tronto writing, "I start from the assumptions about the need for a liberal, democratic, pluralistic society in order for all humans to flourish," and I have to remind myself that the UNFPA (United Nations Population Fund) report on Cairo begins with Development and ends in Finance; that the Beijing platform also and irreducibly mingles the two.[24] Sitting in the UN library auditorium and other public spaces, listening to U.S. women and a sprinkling of patronized "others" talk about global feminist activism, it is dismaying but not surprising to hear, again and again, "follow the money," Mary Beton's cry, which should be interpreted carefully. Woolf's final move now becomes all the more important. The benevolent comparativist impulse in feminism often proceeds in ignorance that societies dreamed of by Tronto can flourish in one part of the world at the expense of another and that capitalism exacerbates this. I therefore fear that the more "late twentieth century [and now twenty-first] American society . . . take[s] seriously . . . the values of caring . . . traditionally associated with woman," the less it will want to learn, under all the garbage of domination and exploitation, those virtues shining in societies where the welfare state is now not allowed to emerge as the barriers between national and international economy are removed; and where, in the name of "gender training," precisely these virtues must be impatiently undermined. To think of learning this from precapitalist formations and yet to help insert them into lines of mobility, we cannot simply be bad-faith emissaries of a globalization that assigns itself the status to train women of "other places" to be women. To be encountered by them as women, we must work to make these other pasts come: "they would come if we worked for them." Not only is this not gender training, it is not even "learning *about* cultures." This is imagining yourself, really letting yourself be imagined (experience that impossibility) without guarantees, by and in another culture, perhaps. Teleopoiesis. Literature is what escapes the system; you cannot speed read it. The figure "is" irreducible.

The ghost dance does not succeed. It can only ever be a productive supplement, interrupting the necessary march of generalization in "the crossing of borders" so that it remembers its limits. It is in this sense that I have called literary training the irony of the social sciences, if irony is understood as permanent parabasis. It is the name of the move by which the collectivity of the Chorus in Attic comedy moves up, again and again, to interrupt the seemingly coherent dramatic *praxis*—Aristotle's word—to inform the public of a structurally different interpretation of the "same" action. (And even here the leader of the Chorus is always on the way to emerging as a singular voice. There is much to be said about this.)

What we are looking at is a persistent structure, for the ghost dance must also be interrupted, by careful scholarship, precisely in the social sciences. One can understand today's world with Woolf's tiny moment of allusion to imperialism, but its enormity can only be gauged if we remember that, even as Mary Beton senior was taking the air on horseback in Bombay, Gandhi was rising in power and the first moves of an independence negotiated with the British were being made. And even that must be supplemented. We must pray to be haunted by the subaltern who was silenced by the movement toward the Gandhi-Irwin pact of 1930, a year after the publication of *A Room of One's Own*. Sumit Sarkar describes the pact as "a sudden retreat" from the original position held by the Indian National Congress, and as a "historical puzzle concerning the change in Gandhi's attitudes [that] cannot be solved in terms of pressure from Liberal leaders alone. . . . There is some evidence that the crucial role was played by [Indian] business pressure."[25] The economic facts would undo a binary opposition between Britain and India.

Such Area Studies–style social scientific research, complicating the textuality of European literature when it touches the global South, would allow us to realize that the literary text in isolation does not lead directly to savvy politics. And in this particular case, such work would show that the undoing of the colonizer/colonized binary by economic fact gives us the genealogy of globalization in its current manifestation, before postcolonialism or liberal multiculturalism began. To supplement Comparative Literature with (comparative) Area Studies allows us to rethink mere national-origin collectivities.

What I have described is an obstinate attempt at a formal

training of the imagination in the classroom. Filling it with substance would take us into the UN and international NGOs, the real players in a dominant feminist collectivity crossing borders—activist comparativism, today. The obvious gap between the two cannot be filled by only academic labor. With that proviso, I turn now to my two literary examples: Tayeb Salih and Mahasweta Devi.

In a rather trivial sense, capitalist imperialism is an effort to win the world for calculation. But the best imperialist calculation is that which is just and restrained by what Jon Elster calls "imperfect rationality": "Man [*sic*] often is not rational, and rather exhibits *weakness of will*. Even when not rational, man knows that he is irrational and can *bind himself* to protect himself against the irrationality. This second-best or imperfect rationality takes care both of reason and of passion."[26] The theme of calculation inspired by a vision of justice underlies Conrad's staging of Marlow as the latter compares Belgian and British imperialisms and justifies the British variety:

> The conquest of the earth, which mostly means the taking it away from those who have a different complexion or slightly flatter noses than ourselves, is not a pretty thing when you look into it too much. What redeems it is the idea only. An idea at the back of it; not a sentimental pretence but an idea; and an uselfish belief in the idea—something you can set up, and bow down before, and offer a sacrifice to.[27]

The requirement for restraint underlies the whole story. Do not "go native," become obliterated in another collectivity. If you must listen to the sirens, have your men bind you to the mast. If you lack such restraint, you will discover how horrible it is to be truly uncivilized.

Disgrace haunts my essay. It is the "real" response to *Heart of Darkness*, showing how, in this historical conjuncture, in a particular place called South Africa, "going native" can be imagined.[28]

Heart of Darkness is an early story about such work: the economic calculus of Belgian imperialism touching the raw edge of response from an Englishman who sees the complicity of the seemingly benevolent British imperialism with it. If to "go native" means to enter the community of others "responsibly," so that responses can follow from both sides, this novel denies the teleopoiesis that can resonate with evil laughter (see note 5).

Literature contains the element of surprising the historical. But it is also true that a literary text produces the effect of being inevitable—indeed, one might argue that that effect is what provokes reading, as transgression of the text. *Heart of Darkness* certainly seems to signal that there was no other way for the British nineteenth century to give us another account of white going native black, although the transgressive moment for levering the text around is there in Marlow's image of "sacrifice" and "bowing down."[29] Since the textuality of Conrad's history with Britain is abundantly available to the reader even of jacket copy, one can construct a theory that the fabula of *Heart of Darkness* legitimizes and delegitimizes at once. For Josef Teodor Konrad Nalecz Korzeniowski "went native" with the British, exclaiming, "the wonder, the wonder" as he wrote so responsibly in a language not his own.[30] The representation, seeming inevitable, asks for transgressive readings. I discuss *Season of Migration to the North* and *Pterodactyl, Puran Sahay and Pirtha* as two such readings.[31]

Politically correct metropolitan multiculturalists want the world's others to be identitarians; nationalist (Jameson) or class (Ahmad). To undo this binary demand is to suggest that peripheral literature may stage more surprising and unexpected maneuvers toward collectivity. Insofar as Salih's and Devi's novels do this, I am calling them transgressive readings of *Heart of Darkness*.

Tayeb Salih also gives us an embedded account of a man who enters the space of another collectivity "responsibly." There is, strictly speaking, no Marlow in *Seasons*. But the anonymous narrator of this first-person narrative is so strongly focalized that it reads like a frame narrative. The action takes place mostly in an unnamed village in the Sudan. The narrator has just returned from Britain. Mustafa Sa'eed, the Kurtz figure, whom our narrator meets in the village, mysteriously disappears toward the beginning of the story. His "narrative" is about his life in Britain and its anticipation and reflection in the postcolonial state of the Sudan. It is Britain that is the "other place" in this novel.

In *Heart of Darkness* the collectivity of the other as well as the collectivity of the same are only vestigially described: Marlow the good loner, standing out among a vestigial community of listeners, and Kurtz the bad loner, placed among a shadowy collection of Afro-colonials and Africans. In *Seasons* both the Sudanese and the British "people" are discriminated in "human" terms. And the bad loner, Mustafa Sa'eed, is allowed to speak—in a reported narrative, as in Conrad's novel, but at much greater length. Here too we have an implicit comparison between two ways of entering other space, but the indeterminate conclusion surprises us. By his own account, Sa'eed entered Britain intellectually and erotically. The unnamed narrator of the novel, who has a British doctorate, significantly enough, in poetry, tells us about the West only once, in the beginning. It should be mentioned that, somewhat like Kurtz, Mustafa is shown to have used his intellectual skills for the benefit of the state—Kurtz the colonial, Mustafa the postcolonial. By contrast, the unnamed narrator is not shown as using his literary-critical skills in any way, except to be able to imagine the European other as human.

Here is the lone passage, thought by the unnamed narrator, about Britain. It comes early in the book, before the reader has encountered Mustafa Sa'eed.

> I preferred not to say . . . that just like us they are born and die, and in the journey from the cradle to the grave they dream dreams some of which come true and some of which are frustrated; that they fear the unknown, search for love and seek contentment in wife and child; that some are strong and some are weak; that some have been given more than they deserve by life, while others have been deprived by it, but that the differences are narrowing and most of the weak are no longer weak. I did not say this to Mahjoub, though I wish I had done so, for he was intelligent; in my conceit I was afraid he would not understand. (SM 3–4)

This passage may well be intertextual with Chinua Achebe's famous comment on *Heart of Darkness*: "It is not the differentness that worries Conrad but the lurking hint of kinship, of common ancestry."[33] Salih's narrator is not "worried" by it but still withholds it, for he is expected by his fellow villagers to be culturally identitarian, fixated on difference from the metropole.

The Salih passage also brings to mind Freud's description of the *Unheimlich*: "in [certain] circumstances the familiar can become uncanny" (UC 220). What is home—to be human in the world—becomes inhospitable, provoking anxiety or *Angst*.

The only other article that Freud had read on this peculiar affect was something by Ernst Jentsch, where the definition ignored the transformative moment. "Jentsch did not get beyond this relation of the uncanny to the novel and unfamiliar," Freud wrote. "Something must first come forth into [*hinkommen*] the new and unfamiliar in order to make it uncanny" (UC 221).

What Salih's narrator feels about Britain is that the people there are like us, familiar. Yet he does not utter this; he interrupts himself. As the novel unfolds, we know that the name of what comes forth to transform this familiar shared humanity of that strange and unfamiliar country called England into a source of fear and anxiety (*Angst*) may be something called "colonialism." We hark back to the passage by Achebe.

Salih's narrator will remain a vehicle of the undecidable. I am suggesting that we should allow peripheral literature this prerogative, not read it with foregone conclusions that deny it literariness.

Salih's narrator seems, then, to be a vehicle of the undecidable. His signature is the interruption. I will mention two important ones here and a third in the next chapter. The first introduces a relaxed conversation among the senior members of the community. The second ends the embedded narrative sequence of the book.

If Conrad's novel is about civility and the savage, Salih's novel obviously shuttles between its displacement: modernity and tradition. If Conrad's novel uses Kurtz's white Intended and black mistress to sharpen the polarity, Salih's novel uses sexual difference as a major shuttle to weave the text in its undecidability, moving from pole to pole.

The first narrative interruption in *A Season* that I will read here interrupts a scene of tradition in its vigor.[33] Older people are respected more in older cultures. This is a conversation about patriarchal heterosex among older villagers, three men and a woman, that crudely objectifies women. The chief interlocutor is the narrator's grandfather, altogether positively valenced by Mustafa Sa'eed—the Kurtz figure in *Seasons*—in the very first reported conversation between Sa'eed and the narrator: " 'Your grandfather knows the secret,' he said to me with that mocking phantom still more in evidence around his eyes" (SM 11). We can thus suspect that, in the world of the novel, we are entering a traditional space that is robust and powerful. And the space of the conversation, in a literal sense, introduces the chapter, through an invocation of a house that overcomes time and becomes, figuratively ("as if"), "natural."

A positive evaluation of culture as a secret or miraculous housing of collectivity opens the chapter, then. The narrator makes an implicit cultural comparison in the matter, precisely, of dwelling, that with which the subject-in-community produces both space (extraterritoriality) and time (the posterior anteriority of memory): "A maze of a house," the long descriptive passage ends, "cool in summer, warm in winter; if one looks objectively at it from outside one feels it to be a frail structure, incapable of survival, but somehow, as if by a miracle, it has surmounted time" (SM 70–71).[34] It should be noted that the word translated as "miracle" here literally means "what cannot be done by human agency."[35]

I have tried to point out that the rhetorical staging of this scene seems to make it signify "tradition." I am not suggesting that the old woman taking part in the discussion is or is not modern or traditional; I am not making a characterological point.[36]

It is this scene of tradition—a relaxed conversation among elders in a timeless house, depicted over four pages with great affect—that the narrator interrupts. The communal scene closes seamlessly over his interruption. The grandfather pays no attention to his entry and picks up the continuing conversation: "'By God, that's some story of yours, Wad Rayyes'" (SM 74). The conversation, following near-pornographic lines, culminates in the old woman—Bint Majzoub—silencing Wad Rayyes with these words: "Wad Rayyes, you're a man who talks rubbish. Your whole brain's in the head of your penis and the head of your penis is as small as your brain" (SM 84). The word for "penis" that she uses comes not from the colloquial Sudanese or from the modern Arabic lingua franca. It is not from the language of pornography or from street slang. It is drawn from the archaic vocabulary of erotica.

Over against this scene are two or three scenes that index "modernity." The most obvious one is ostentatiously layered in multiple reportage, as I schematize below:

Mustafa Sa'eed's widow is courted by the very Wad Rayyes who was the butt of the old woman's contempt and is obliged to marry him. She kills him as he is attempting to consummate the marriage and then kills herself. Mahjoub (the character from whom the initial sentiments about common humanity had also been withheld) is unable to understand that the news of this revenge and suicide is important enough to be the central topic of the conversation between the narrator and himself. Embedded in that realization, the text halts the story in an extended memory of a conference not reported to Mahjoub, who, by the narrator's estimation, represents the kind of rural collectivity that would not be able to understand the postcolonial politics of such conferences. Within this memory we are offered Mustafa Sa'eed's remark, reported by a cabinet minister who is carefully established as belonging to the general corruption and unreliability of the postcolonial national government. Here's the passage, formally disqualified from being "proof" of Salih's misogyny: "He," says the minister, meaning Mustafa Sa'eed, "used to say 'I'll liberate Africa with my . . . ,' and he laughed so widely you could see the arse of his throat" (SM 120).

Again, I am following a rudimentary narratological line here, looking at the way bits of narrative (sequences) are arranged to deliver meaning. Such a method would suggest that the direct description and dialogue of the sequence containing the conversation in the old house and the multiple framing and layered reporting of this sequence signify a contrast that it would be plausible to index as "tradition" versus "modernity." This is not a discussion of characterization or cultural information. In the original, unlike Bint Majzoub, the old woman, neither Mustafa Sa'eed nor the postcolonial functionary is able to pronounce the word for "penis." The translation ignores this differentiation. The Arabic text has nothing but a series of dots, and the coarse expression about the throat is inadequately translated, "the back of the throat." Thus the gender division of freedom of speech between tradition and modernity is made rhetorically unclear in the translation. In the original, the old woman says "penis," the modern man not. Thus, in the book's staging of the two "uses" of the word "penis," "tradition" provides the older woman the possibility of using a word in the private sphere that modernity does not allow the man in the public sphere. Again, I am reading the logic of the rhetoric, not the text as cultural information. It is as if the word "penis," not just any word, after all, uttered in one sequence and marked by its decent withholding in the other, prevents us from making a too-quick conclusion about gender, freedom of speech, and modernity. And the two incidents are pivotal in the story, as well.

The judgment of "modernity" upon Wad Rayyes in terms of narrative logic is rather different from Bint Majzoub's judgment. Wad Rayyes is killed by Mustafa Sa'eed's widow as he marriage-rapes her. The text recodes his vaunted sexual prowess on her body as male violence.

Yet the novel will not decide if, for the space of the novel, that recoding is an unquestioned advance in gender justice. We cannot forget that Mustafa Sa'eed's widow has perhaps acceded to a sense of female (if not proto-feminist) individuality as a result of *his* violence with white women. He has violated and killed a few. She is the only woman in the text who is called by her full proper name: Hosna bint Mahmoud. But, in the logic of the text, there is also the judgment of that other woman who is at least given a real first name, no one's daughter (Bint), no one's mother (Um), but simply Mabrouka, Wad Rayyes's first wife, and a distant cousin of the professor's daughter in *Disgrace*:

> "Good riddance!" she said and went back to sleep, and we could hear her snoring while we were busy preparing Bint Mahmoud for burial. When the people returned from the burial, we found Mabrouka sitting drinking her morning coffee. When some of the women wanted to commiserate with her she yelled, "Women, let everyone of you go about her business. Wad Rayyes dug his grave with his own hands, and Bint Mahmoud, God's blessings be upon her, paid him out in full." Then she gave trilling cries of joy. Yes, by God, my child, she gave trilling cries of joy. (SM 128)

In these trills, Salih's text signals the possibility of a women's collectivity "to come," where a rejection of internalized gendering (in this case unquestioning loyalty to a spouse) will not necessarily be a product of a formulaic "modernity" identified with contact with the West.[37]

Let us look now at the second interruption. In the first part of the book, the narrator remembers Mustafa Sa'eed telling him about an exotic orientalist room he had created in London for the seduction of white women. In the next-to-the-last chapter the narrator enters a room in Sa'eed's village home that is its exact opposite, an English room with a fireplace and a library of English-language political texts. In this room, and without the plausibility of obvious flashback, the dead Mustafa Sa'eed's narrative voice resumes unexpectedly, telling the story of the murder of a white woman, his previous wife, as the successful completion of an act of sex. The narrator interrupts: "I left him talking and went out. I did not let him complete the story" (SM 166). How much a reader will contrive a so-called logical explanation for this, since Mustafa Sa'eed is dead in the story, depends on how practiced or at ease the reader is with the fictive, how much she or he has of what is often called "literary competence." "Practiced *or* at ease"—please note the alternative; it is not always learned, but it can be taught. All we need note here is that, if the narrator is an interruptive agent in the traditional scene I reported above, so is he here in the scene of the violence of the encounter with "modernity." In both cases, it is an interruption—unmotivated and noncharacterological—not an acceptance or rejection of communal collectivity or individualism. The narrator is not indexed as representative of a "Third World" collectivity of culture (Jameson) or class (Ahmad). You do not have to go to Europe to find a Marlow, distanced from Kurtz—as this narrator is from Sa'eed. As a "character," this narrator does not like Sa'eed. As if to emphasize this, another, simpler interruption is staged: "There was no limit to his egoism and his conceit," the narrator thinks. "Despite everything, he wanted history to immortalize him. But I do not have the time to proceed further with this farce. . . . At the break of dawn tongues of fire will devour these lies. Jumping to my feet, I raised the candlelight to the oil painting" (SM 154). He interrupts himself. "I had put out the candles and locked the door of the room. Another fire would not have done any good" (SM 166). Mustafa Sa'eed's story played out in an interim time with no staged listener. The reader has to deal with the fact that it is reported speech outside the encompassing frame of the novel that is silently resumed in the last section. It is an a-chrony that keeps the event's status narratologically undecidable.[38]

I will finally report on the scene where men and women do come together, a scene that comes earlier in the novel. It too is a staged interruption. It is a scene of the Bedouin, the very type of a nomadic prenational collectivity.[39] Their space is carefully tabulated as constructed by the fractured relationship between precolonial and postcolonial geography: "The tribes of El-Mirisab, El-Hawaweer and El-Kababeesh; the judges, resident and itinerant; the Commissioner of North Kordofan, the Commissioner of the Southern North Province, the Commissioner of East Khartoum; the shepherds at the watering places; the Sheikhs and the Nazirs; the Bedouin in hair tents at the intersections of the valleys" (SM 110). In Salih's novel as in Maryse Condé's, colonized collectivity is fractured by the subaltern, here the desert Bedouin rather than the rural gentry or the urban sophisticate.

The Bedouin men are also carefully docketed as impervious to the specificity of women, just like the representative Mahjoub but unlike our narrator, who holds himself apart: "They said that a woman from the tribe of El-Mirisab had killed her husband and the government was in the process of arresting her. . . . I said to them that she had not killed him but that he had died from sunstroke—just as Isabella Seymour had died, and Sheila Greenwood, Ann Hammond, and Jean Morris." (These are the names of Mustafa Sa'eed's English mistresses and wives, all

dead, the last murdered by him.) "Nothing happened," the narrator continues. "No use. No sense of wonder" (SM 110–111).

It is within this frame, in a chapter in the novel whose time
is simply the time of a yet-unexplained exception—"But this
time I was, for no particular reason, in a hurry, so I chose to
go the shortest way" (SM 105)—that an inter-diction of sexual
difference is staged. The hurry is because Mustafa Sa'eed's
widow has killed Wad Rayyes—her husband under duress—and
herself, but the reader does not know it. Hence all that he or
she knows is that the scene is interstitial, interruptive of the
narrative stream. The scene itself is doubly interruptive. At first
the men imitate women. And then "the light and the clamour
attracted the Bedouin from the neighbouring wadi ravines and
foothills, both men and women, people whom you would not
see by day, when it was just as if they melted away under the
light of the sun. . . . At that time and place they were beautiful"
(SM 114). Here too is a women's collectivity, again unconnected to a (past) present, as the possibility of collectivity in
Mabrouka's trills of joy are unconnected to a (future) present. I
have not much interest in diagnosing Salih's sexual politics. For
the kind of institutional literary pedagogy I am envisaging, do
not accuse—do not excuse—turn around through reading and
use remains the imperative.[40] And these two moments—perhaps
of textual transgression—remain useful for thinking a gendered
collectivity that unsettles a more binary opposition of tradition
(Bedouin woman) and modernity (Bint Mahmoud).

The scene of the dance is more than a mingling of men and
women in the improvisation of a song that uses traditional structure for the instant, a millennial characteristic of orality. This is
the only section of the novel in colloquial Sudanese. This "tribal" moment is the only "present" in the history of the language.
But it is also a subaltern framing of the traditional instant in the
modern as temporary: the men and women dance upon the tem-

porary stage of the blazing headlights of a circle of trucks. We will relate this to the thematics of the text of collectivity.

I will pick up this novel again in the next chapter. For now let me add an interim closure. It is quite unnecessary to revisit what was a well-meaning effort on the part of Fredric Jameson in his by now notorious essay, "Third World Literature in the Era of Multinational Capitalism."[41] The only point I want to make here is that Jameson was generalizing from China, as his chief critic, Aijaz Ahmad, was arguing from a species of muscular Marxism, which automatically substitutes class for nationality. A careful reading of literature coming out of "the Third World," with attention to language and idiom and respect for their grafting, will show that the inevitable themes of tradition and modernity, collectivity and individualism may be in play in many different ways. I have tried to show this by reading Salih reading Conrad. This is a project that fits the new Comparative Literature.

I will close by looking at a moment in Mahasweta Devi's *Pterodactyl*, a novella on which I have written more extensively elsewhere.

Devi's novel is not a self-conscious response to Conrad. I choose to read it thus because it is the story of a journey into the heart(land) of the other.

Puran Sahay is a middle-class Hindu Indian journalist who is staged as limited in many ways. This is the man who travels to aboriginal country. As in Salih's novel, there are postcolonial government functionaries and nongovernmental employees at work here, just as in *Heart of Darkness* the sorry structure of Belgian imperialism is at work in the Congo. Puran enters the other's space "responsibly," as did Mustafa Sa'eed and, indeed, Kurtz.

Am I, unwittingly, creating a taxonomy here? Perhaps I am.

Kurtz is shown as succumbing to the horror of touching humanity in the raw: "Exterminate all the brutes!" (HD 84). Mustafa Sa'eed is shown as unable to survive an individual phallogocentric project to undo the difference between the colonizer and the colonized. In the process, Salih excavates colonized space to show its heterogeneity. In Mahasweta's story, Puran is accepted by the Aboriginals, and it is they who play subject.

If Salih postpones sexual difference and the consequent possibility of collectivity maximally, Mahasweta does so minimally. Puran is shown to be incapable of sustaining a relationship with a particular woman from his own (middle) class, limned respectfully as an agent of affect and intellect. All the good government officials have active or activist wives who are elsewhere. The aboriginal women are shown to be as impervious to government family planning posters as are the Bedouin to women's specificity. In the absence of any infrastructural effort at education and of a structure of welfare, children are sold, with devastating affective consequences. The harshness of the necessity to distance aboriginal sexuality is reflected in a cruel metaphor: "The infants rest their faces like ticks on the chests of the skeleton mothers" (PT 128).

We are, then, in an effortfully established rather than effortlessly generalized male scene. I have done harm to the novella by quickly summarizing many delicate rhetorical moves. I add to that by giving you the answer before considering the staging of the failure of response. Puran's arrival is coincident with the coming of the rains. The area had been suffering from a drought that had led to devastation that the government was having difficulty technically designating as "famine."[42] Those so-called "difficulties" are part of the story. Puran is included into the Aboriginals' mythic and collective self-representation as the bringer of rain.

Now in the case of Maryse Condé's representation of multilingual subaltern Africa, and in the case of the rhetoricity of the structure of interpretation, I have spoken of "literary competence." In the case of how the below crosses to the above, I have spoken of "restricted permeability." As we proceed to rearrange institutionally, in the name of a new Comparative Literature, what can only happen perhaps in an unnameable future, we can include a rigorous awareness of a restricted permeability within a notion of literary competence. I demonstrate, in altogether broad strokes, below.

Subaltern aboriginal groups read "nature" with uncanny precision. Their weather predictions, altogether confined in geographical scope, are always astonishing to someone less used to living in the eco-biome. The fictive nature of their inclusion of Puran as rainmaker is therefore more complex than a lack of "scientific" savvy. Mahasweta stages this complexity thus: the general narrative is that Bikhia, an aboriginal lad, has drawn the picture of a pterodactyl. Puran Sahay, a nonaboriginal radical journalist, has come to investigate. Of nonaboriginal Indians he is the only one who gains entry into the uncertain "presence" of the ancient bird. But before that encounter, which is the staging of a nonencounter, Puran is taken into the collectivity of the aboriginal other. If Kurtz and Mustafa Sa'eed have "gone native," it is the native who welcomes Puran, as the rainmaker. We should think of the elusive appearance and disappearance of the Bedouin and mark the hybridity and heterogeneity in Salih's and Mahasweta's texts, if read with the linguistic attention that is the hallmark of Comparative Literature.

Here is the scene, given at first in the indirect free style that signals Puran's thought world. Notice that this too is a question. "Bikhia has received his ancestral soul. . . . What has Puran received? Bikhia keeps pulling him outside and points ahead. Water is running down a crack in the rock. Bikhia looks at him in deep expectation" (PT 143–144).

I think the reader is obliged to surmise that Puran is expected to offer a response here. But he cannot come through. "Is Bikhia asking him to listen to the music of the waters? Puran understands nothing." This is the staging of the missed moment when Puran becomes responsible by not being able to respond. He understands later, in a deliberate representation of a non sequitur.

"Caves, cave paintings, Bikhia's picture. Puran understands at this time, that rainfall on the night of his arrival may give birth to a saying" (PT 144). There is no obvious logical or syntactic connection between the two sentences. And the word for "saying" is, literally, "what is [a person] saying[?]"—a tiny question lexically frozen into a noun, as if ordinary language allows even the object of his understanding to be only a question behaving like an object.

The intending subject fails to answer correctly when a response has already been entered into myth. This is the structure that can open entry into responsibility with the subaltern other, whose definition then rests in an irreducible figure—"cave, cave paintings." Mahasweta gives us the diagnostic confidence of the postcolonial Indian Harisharan, part of the representative "Indian" collective national identity, full of goodwill, a devoted local government worker who has not earned the right to responsibility. He comes to "Nature" by way of an English self-help book. For Puran, the "real" subaltern is now in figures, "cave paintings."

"Man," he begins with the English word, "as a result of [the ancestor's shadow—the pterodactyl] whole villages were awash with death-wish"—the English word again. "Night before last I couldn't sleep, couldn't eat, what a night of bad dreams! . . . My wife bought Benjamin's *Everyday Nature Cure* for me. . . . What does *Nature Cure* say?" Puran asks. It is crucial for Puran now to find out what Nature says. The word for "Nature" that Mahasweta uses in the last quoted sentence, a representation of Puran thinking, is the Bengali *prakriti*. It is not that Devi is "against English." In fact it is plausible that a middle-class Bengali should pepper his conversation with English words. English is in a differential here with Puran's Bengali, indicating, perhaps, something like a failure of responsible communication with the aboriginal for the relatively benevolent postcolonial collectivity represented by Harisharan. Puran is a loner. It is the difference rather than some substantive linguistic preference that seems important here.

It surely cannot be without significance that it is from Harisharan that the confident description comes: "Man! [in English] People who have nothing need *miracles* [in English again]. For now it's through you . . . now a story will become song . . . and the song will enter the history that they hold in their oral ballads" (PT 144–145).

Letting go of control leads Puran to the space of the other, where no "human" can "go native." This is no mortal's ghost. It is a pterodactyl that has appeared. We will look at its coming and going in the next chapter. For now, an invocation, again, of begging the question of collectivity. The new Comparative Literature must ask, again and again, "How many are we?" "Who are they?" as the narrative of *Seasons*, and of Puran, Bikhia, and the pterodactyl detach themselves from generalizations of collective identity. Reading these texts with attention to language and idiom, Comparative Literature supplements the apparitions of Cultural and Ethnic Studies as well as the arrogance of Area Studies where it retains the imprints of the Cold War.

Why have I written largely of women to launch the question of the recognition of ceaselessly shifting collectivities in our disciplinary practice? Because women are not a special case, but can represent the human, with the asymmetries attendant upon any such representation. As simple as that.

CHAPTER 3

PLANETARITY

All through these pages I have suggested that literary studies must take the "figure" as its guide. The meaning of the figure is undecidable, and yet we must attempt to dis-figure it, read the logic of the metaphor. We know that the figure can and will be literalized in yet other ways. All around us is the clamor for the rational destruction of the figure, the demand for not clarity but immediate comprehensibility by the ideological average. This destroys the force of literature as a cultural good. Anyone who believes that a literary education should still be sponsored by universities must allow that one must learn to read. And to learn to read is to learn to dis-figure the undecidable figure into a responsible literality, again and again. It is my belief that initiation into cultural explanation is a species of such a training in reading. By abandoning our commitment to reading, we unmoor the connection between the humanities and cultural instruction.

In this chapter I will argue that, as presumed collectivities cross borders under the auspices of a Comparative Literature supplemented by Area Studies, they might attempt to figure themselves—imagine themselves—as planetary rather than continental, global, or worldly. The planet is easily claimed. Let me explain what effort is implicit in my invocation of that word.

I propose the planet to overwrite the globe. Globalization is the imposition of the same system of exchange everywhere. In the gridwork of electronic capital, we achieve that abstract ball covered in latitudes and longitudes, cut by virtual lines, once the equator and the tropics and so on, now drawn by the requirements of Geographical Information Systems. To talk planet-talk by way of an unexamined environmentalism, referring to an undivided "natural" space rather than a differentiated political space, can work in the interest of this globalization in the mode of the abstract as such. (I have been insisting that to transmute the literatures of the global South to an undifferentiated space of English rather than a differentiated political space is a related move.) The globe is on our computers. No one lives there. It allows us to think that we can aim to control it. The planet is in the species of alterity, belonging to another system; and yet we inhabit it, on loan. It is not really amenable to a neat contrast with the globe. I cannot say "the planet, on the other hand." When I invoke the planet, I think of the effort required to figure the (im)possibility of this underived intuition.[1]

To be human is to be intended toward the other. We provide for ourselves transcendental figurations of what we think is the origin of this animating gift: mother, nation, god, nature. These are names of alterity, some more radical than others. Planet-thought opens up to embrace an inexhaustible taxonomy of such names, including but not identical with the whole range of human universals: aboriginal animism as well as the spectral white mythology of postrational science. If we imagine ourselves as planetary subjects rather than global agents, planetary creatures rather than global entities, alterity remains underived from us; it is not our dialectical negation, it contains us as much as it flings us away. And thus to think of it is already to transgress, for, in spite of our forays into what we metaphorize, differently, as outer and inner space, what is above and beyond our own reach is not continuous with us as it is not, indeed, specifically discontinuous. We must persistently educate ourselves into this peculiar mindset.

It is often pointed out that globalization, in the form of ancient world systems, has a long history. This historical reckoning remains crucial to our task. In the relatively autonomous economic sphere, however, information technology has also created a rupture—hence my invocation of the computerized globe.

I began this book with academic memos. It is by way of such unremarkable moves that cultural instruction hopes to shift the episteme. Indeed, those memos were attempting to deal with changes in the student body because disciplines that had started in the aftermath of war were now in a globalizing world. It is as an alternative to such timid and placatory gestures, as well to the arrogance of the cartographic reading of world lit. in translation as the task of Comparative Literature, that I propose the planet.

Is this to render our home uncanny? I am, of course, not thinking of the English word "uncanny," but of the Stracheys' translation of Freud's word *unheimlich*, signifying the turning of what is homey into something *unheimlich*—uncanny in this German-substitute sense. To think the word this way is in itself a disciplinary exercise in Comparative Literature: "In what circumstances the familiar can become uncanny and frightening, I shall show in what follows. . . . What is *heimlich* thus comes to be *unheimlich*" (UC 220, 224).

Some years ago, writing on the work of the subaltern studies collective, I had commented, "the figure of woman is pervasively instrumental in the shifting of the function of discursive systems."[2] We will see below that the figure of woman-as-mother-as-vagina is important in Freud's explanation of the uncanny. In our attempt to track planetarity as making our home *unheimlich* or uncanny, we will construct an allegory of reading where the discursive system shifts from vagina to planet as the signifier of the uncanny, by way of nationalist colonialism and postcoloniality. This is in keeping with my method: gender as a general critical instrument rather than something to be factored in in special cases.

In a peculiar passage in "The Uncanny," Freud finds the normative confirming definition of the *Unheimlich* in what is uttered by some abnormal men:

> If it does not rest upon mere coincidence, [this instance] furnishes a beautiful confirmation of our theory of the uncanny. It often happens that neurotic men explain that they feel there is something uncanny about the female genital organs. This *unheimlich* place, however, is the entrance to the former *Heim* [home] of all human beings, to the place where each one of us lived once upon a time and in the beginning. (UC 245)

As is so often the case, Freud discloses himself managing a crisis even as he (rationally) diagnoses the crisis management as a
neurosis and derives the reason of psychoanalysis from it.

This triple whammy is made visible in Luce Irigaray's feminist psychoanalytic reading of Plato.[3] Reading many details in
the Greek text, she shows that the allegory of the cave, by constructing a disavowed womb (with an unacknowledged paraphragmatic hymen) as a place where we are and that we can
escape, fulfills the dream-wish of reason to wish away the
inescapable control exercised by the uncanny. Her mesmerizing,
repetitive, cyclical reading mimes the structure of transference
and countertransference. The aim of psychoanalysis is to access
the subject to strengthen the agent—to tap the psychic apparatus to restore social viability. In keeping with this, Irigaray ana-
lyzes Plato not to dismantle him but to restore social agency to
the dreamer. Acknowledge the presence of the paraphragmatic
way out, acknowledge the vagina as the portal of birth written
into your cave and then . . . you will see that what you see as rupture is also a repetition, the saving myth of the death of the
scapegoat—Socrates, the man who escapes and returns—rather
than only the singular risk of the escape into reason.

I want to create a loose homology here between Irigaray's
method in this early essay and the method of the new Area
Studies as it works with Comparative Literature and Eth-
nic/Cultural Studies. In her careful work with language, helping read the dream of reason with sympathy in order to harness the dreamer to institutional agency, Irigaray becomes our
mediator—the feminist reader rather than an analyst within
the institutional situation. I have always been wary of choosing
psychoanalysis "as such" (if there can be such a thing) as the
model of reading.

Over against such a readerly choice—questioning "experience" as a text to be read in the interest of agency—is the pecu-

liar American strength of Ethnic Studies, which will not let go of "the authority of experience" as the bedrock of its theorizing. The first wave of literary feminism in the United States, well before the institutional emergence of Ethnic Studies, worked from this strength. I am thinking, of course, of Susan Gubar and Sandra Gilbert's monumental work *The Madwoman in the Attic*, which belongs to the same era as Chinua Achebe's "Image of Africa" and "Plato's *Hystera*."[4] Confrontational, experiential, and in effect monolingual, harnessing the ethereality of theory where available, today's Ethnic Studies carries this trait. It must now learn to play with Area Studies, emphasizing the textuality of the language of "ethnic origin," producing that inter-dictive "and yet" when either patient polyglot transference (Irigaray) or impatient dismissal (Gilbert and Gubar) seems to appropriate center stage.

It is with such cautions in mind that I begin to track the figuration of the uncanny in the three texts we read in the last chapter: *Heart of Darkness, Season of Migration in the North, Pterodactyl*. I stay with the abnormal yet normative confirmation of the definitive: "the female genital organs . . . this *unheimlich* place . . . is the entrance to the former *Heim* of all human beings."

I closed the last chapter by saying that feminist presuppositions could be generalized, with no more than the usual specificity problems. Now, with the help of Irigaray's reading method on Plato, I am going to use a general feminist take on Freud to make my point about making home uncanny.

The reading goes like this: Freud's rethinking of the mind-body problem was extraordinary, the production of the psychologically available mind as the work (and being) of a psychologically unavailable (metapsychological) apparatus—much as the sentient body is the production of a materially unavailable physiological working out of the body's materiality.

Indeed the two are linked in ways that can be deciphered. This is the good part. This brilliant morphology is shackled, however, to a family story specific to a time, place, class, gender—supported by the kind of cultural props such specificities would provide.[5] As Irigaray attempted to wrest the Platonic text from its narrative commitments, so do we attempt to separate the Freudian text from the narrative that it inhabits.

How does it figure here? I will give the most mechanical outline and ask the reader to understand that the way I got here was far from mechanical.

The *Heimlich/Unheimlich* relationship is indeed, formally, the defamiliarization of familiar space. But its substantive type does not have to be the entrance to the vagina. Colonialism, decolonization, and postcoloniality involved special kinds of traffic with people deemed "other"—the familiarity of a presumed common humanity defamiliarized, as it were. I am not suggesting that there is a necessary connection between these politicoeconomic phenomena and the specific image that figures the uncanny for Freud and his patients. I am recording a certain difference in the figuration that I noticed as I read these three novels.

Heart of Darkness is committed to the narrative of nation as expanding space: that story is told in the broad strokes of male bonding and a loner escaping that bond. The gender figuration follows Freud's own culturally permitted narrative and the substantive type seems to remain intact. *Season* undoes the polarizing of colonizing and colonized space, and, curiously enough, it is the sense of male bonding that is undermined. In my reading, the narrative undoes stereotyped gender presuppositions to undo the polarization. And the fixed signification of the type of the uncanny comes to be destabilized. *Pterodactyl* courts planetarity, and the defamiliarization of home does not carry the class-gendered meaning at all. Who knows how much of this is my transactionality as reader? Does one ever know? I have tried to be as scrupulous as possible. I take psychoanalysis as a kind of lexicon, of course; I cannot psychoanalyze Conrad or his text.[6] I am taking Freud's canny cultured European male notion of the type of the uncanny as an allegory of reading. I read the staging of *Heart of Darkness* as a classic representation of the (ab)normal definition of the *(Un)heimlich*. I can therefore give a feminist spin to Achebe's comment on the anxiety produced by the familiar humanity of the African. The text must reverse the values of nature, turn "natural" semiotics around as the backdrop of this uncanny humanity: "There was no joy in the brilliance of sunshine," Marlow remembers, "and this stillness of life did not resemble a peace" (HD 55, 56).[7] I can learn about the management of "the former home of all human beings" from the structural representation of that dark heart. Not only a heart but also the mouth of the vagina; as, in Plato's dream, not only a cave but also the mouth of the vagina.

Of course one would need a careful reading to secure this. I find that I have been more than usually schematic in this chapter, perhaps because I cannot offer a formulaic access to planetarity. No one can.

From pages 19 to 22 in my paperback edition, the book describes the steamer trip from Bordeaux to "the mouth of the big river." The trek to the Company's Station takes another eight pages. On page 31, Marlow leaves "with a caravan of sixty men, for a two-hundred-mile tramp" to the Central Station. The heart of the story is the eight-hundred-mile voyage to see Kurtz, "the chief of the Inner Station" (HD 40). A little later, there is a description of a glimpse of "the great river . . . glittering . . . through a sombre gap" that is as close to the scare of the Kantian dynamic sublime as you can get. There is talk of something being in there and something coming out of there: "What was in there? I could see a little ivory coming out of there, and I had heard Mr. Kurtz was in there." From this vagina dentata we go another step. The interim sixty pages develop the anxiety of this place of "prehistoric humanity," and on page 103 we see in the black woman an image of that uncanny that gives witness to the soul and gaze of that first dwelling place: "the colossal body of the fecund and mysterious life seemed to look at her, pensive, as though it had been looking at the image of its own tenebrous and passionate soul."

I have tried to show that the rhetoric of Salih's novel gives us a critique of colonialism and anticolonialism as traffic in the reproductive politics of sexual difference. His text also turns to the definitive uncanny in the end. The narrator enters the river, in a hardly avoidable symbology of the womb, "naked as my mother bore me." The interruption of Mustafa Sa'eed's story takes place, in narrative time, *after* this plunge, and *after* the story has already come to its appropriate conclusion at the end of the previous section. The plunge in the river is an uncanny space of time. The narrator now declares, "I did not let him complete the story" (SM 166). In this mode of performative contradiction, the narrator interrupts his death in these uncanny waters by the most banal longing for fire, a cigarette, a little cigar, quite clearly not just a cigarette at this point. In two echoing sentences, rocking between choice and decision, he "chooses life" (SM 168). The translation spoils the comical parallel of the two sentences. The very last sentence likens the narrator to a comic actor, shouting "Help! Help!" [*nejda*] in a classical Arabic translation of English or French, rather than the more colloquial "help me" [*sa'iduni*] that would have been more appropriate in the mouth of a drowning man. What does this ending mean? At least a rejection of the heavy postcolonial thematic, marked by sexual difference, that is the legacy of *Heart of Darkness*.

In Mahasweta Devi's novella the womb is not a place of fear, although the metaphor is as obvious as in Conrad or Salih. "Now go down through a roofless tunnel, down, down, go down, turn, enter a dark cave again. The sound of water above them and its floor is slippery . . ." (PT 175), and so on. But the question of sexual difference has been bracketed, as we have seen. And there is nothing initially familiar about the pterodactyl that the force of the narrative could render uncanny. The paintings on the cave wall could be either ancient or contemporary. Puran doesn't care.

The pterodactyl remains other; it cannot dwell, nor can it be buried. The impossible death of the ghost is no more than an occasion for "responsibility" between members of two groups that would otherwise be joined by the abstract collectivity of Indian citizenship: the Hindu and the aboriginal. The uncanny is planetary here, not in play as a stake in sexual difference.

The novella is embedded in a critique of the postcolonial state and a declaration of love for the historical other of the entire legal collectivity of the Indian nation. Indeed, the fig-ure of the pterodactyl can claim the entire planet as its other. It is prior to our thinking of continents: "When the conti-nents drifted again and took their current shape . . . you were supposed to have become extinct" (PT 156). It is a figure of the mindset that can make the "new" Comparative Literature work. The appropriations of Jurassic Park into cyberpunk may have rendered that thought silly. One will have to look out for what Raymond Williams calls the preemergent around the corner, suppressed by a specifically metropolitan moment that emphasizes the uneven and asymmetrical global digital divide. The "preemergent" leads us toward a "structure of feeling." Raymond Williams thought and wrote in a way that could take on board the less foundational modes of thought implied by Marxism and made explicit by Freud and Foucault.

But thinking of institutional attitudes to be fostered by pedagogy, we do not need to tap those modes, we need only remember them. The altered attitudes toward language learning, areas versus nation-states, figure versus rational expectations, that I have been discussing in these chapters can no doubt be plotted as a "structure of feeling," if that is the language we prefer. The scenario that I am constructing would suggest that the dominant figuring of "prehistory" as cyberpresent or science fiction adventure would interfere with the emergence of the figuration of an undecidable planetary alterity. We must therefore observe the figuration of that pre-emergent in this text, and experience the "structure of feeling" as a narrative of the impossible.

The *Heart of Darkness* theme belongs to European national colonialisms. In this overly schematic last chapter, a few other bases must be touched. We must remember the older U.S. marginalities: Hispanic, African; and the heritage of older empires: Russian, Ottoman, Habsburg. I will remain caught in the scandal of Comparative Literature, unable to access First Nation orality. I mention my shortcoming in hope. Postcolonialism remained caught in mere nationalism over against colonialism. Today it is planetarity that we are called to imagine—to displace this historical alibi, again and again. I outline this utopian idea as a task for thinking ground because otherwise a "reformed" comparative literary vision may remain caught within varieties of cultural relativism, specular alterity, and cyber-benevolence. Transnational literacy may remain confined within a politics of recognizing multiculturalism or of international aid, in the interest of a "Development" of which the promise of cyber-literacy is increasingly a part. This is, indeed, a general representation of the politicized edge of any comparative discipline in the United States. I am in general solidarity with this. But as in the case of crossing borders, my solidarity is critical. I cannot ignore Donald Pease's judgment that metropolitan multiculturalism—the latter phase of dominant postcolonialism—precomprehends U.S. manifest destiny as transformed asylum for the rest of the world. As Pease suggests, on the basis of much empirical detail: "In restricting the referentiality of the term 'post-colonial' to the political settlements that took place after the decolonization of former European colonies, postcolonial theory has constructed the most recent of the variations on the theme of U.S. exceptionalism."[8] Indeed, this position, the United States as the final and hospitable home of cultural rights, seems to me to be closer to an enhanced metropolitan nationalism than to the necessary impossibility of a "grounding" in planetarity. This is the most immediate short circuit that a comparativist universalism, shuttling between Area Studies and Ethnic/Cultural Studies, might trip. This for me is therefore the most immediate agenda item for the study of race and ethnicity. Here anthropology is deflected through mere identity claims in a simulacrum of the project of other-ing the subject. For if anthropology classically studies the other as community, Ethnic/ Cultural Studies cathects the community as "others." But given the ruling ideology of "the authority of experience," we may be in danger of seeking the community as no more than a collection of ourselves.[9]

In 1990, a time that seems remote from the urges that make me undertake this work, I wrote about ethnicity as follows. I had a clear sense that I was writing not as a comparativist but in the paradisciplinary tendency inhabited by discourses of identity:

It is through the literature of ethnicity that we customarily approach the question of globality within literary-cultural studies defined along humanist disciplinary lines. The word *ethnos* in Greek meant "one's *own* kind of people" and therefore we take it to mean, by extension, "nation." Side by side with the Greek word *ethnos* in the Greek-English Lexicon is the word *ethnikos*—other people, often taken to mean "heathen, pagan." . . . I think the literature of ethnicity writes itself between *ethnos*—a writer writing for her *own* people (whatever that means) without deliberated self-identification as such—and *ethnikos*, the pejoratively defined other reversing the charge, (de)anthropologizing herself by separating herself into a staged identity. The literature of ethnicity in this second sense thus carries, paradoxically, the writer's signature as divided against itself.[10]

In 1996, Derrida wrote as follows:

What is identity, this concept of which the transparent identity to itself is always dogmatically presupposed by so many debates on monoculturalism or multiculturalism, nationality, citizenship, and belonging, in general? And before the identity of the subject, what is *ipseity*? The latter is not reducible to an abstract capacity to say "I," which it will always have preceded. Perhaps it signifies, in the first place, the power of an "I can," which is more originary than the "I" in a chain where the "*pse*" of *ipse* no longer allows itself to be dissociated from power . . . mastery and sovereignty.[11]

Two kinds of points are being made in the Derrida text: first, that the ethnos is already self-divided, and second, that ipseity or self-sameness has something in common with the despot—*pse* reversed—claiming power and property. Identity politics is neither smart nor good. Comparative Literature laced with Area Studies goes rather toward the other.

All my examples so far have been postcolonial, tied to New Immigrant groups in the United States: Maryse Condé, J. M. Coetzee, Tayeb Salih, Mahasweta Devi; with Conrad as control. Cultural Studies is heavily invested in New Immigrant groups. It seems to me that a planetary Comparative Literature must attempt to move away from this base. What I write in closing will give some indication of the way out, as far as a nonexpert can imagine it. These words are no more than scattered speculations, to mark the limits of my rather conventional U.S. Comparative Literature training: English, French, German, poetry and literary theory, romantic and modernist.

As I hope above, the new Comparative Literature will touch the older minorities: African, Asian, Hispanic. It will take in its sweep the new postcoloniality of the post-Soviet sector and the special place of Islam in today's breaking world. Not everything for everyone, all at once. But a Comparative Literature format—historical and linguistic—possible, for any slice chosen from any of these places, the background filled in by new reference tools on Franco Moretti's model.

I am writing these words in Hong Kong. I come here as often as I can, and go on to other Chinas, to get a sense of the immensely changeful and vast scenario of the evolving Asia–Pacific. The three papers I heard from Wu Hung this time would be a way into the Comparative Literature of the future, if seen through the eyes of a critic for whom gender is not just for special cases.[12] This is no more than an example, of course, and it touches only the People's Republic of China. The Asia–Pacific spans Southeast Asia, Micronesia, Polynesia, New Zea-

land, perhaps Australia, Hawai'i, California—each with different histories of the movements of power. It is with this ensem-
ble that the divided and diversified story of Asian America, old
and new immigrants, must be imaginatively cobbled to make for
a robust Comparative Literature. The time for producing historically thin "theory" describing the feeling of migrants in
pseudopsychoanalytic vocabulary is over. It was exhausted in the
first phase of the Comparative Literature dispute reflected in the
Bernheimer collection.

The old postcolonial model—very much "India" plus the
Sartrian "Fanon"—will not serve now as the master model for
transnational to global cultural studies on the way to planetarity. We are dealing with heterogeneity on a different scale and
related to imperialisms on another model:

> Over the time that the world has known substantial
> states . . . empires have been the dominant and largest
> state form. . . . Only now . . . do we seem to be leaving
> the age of massive Eurasian empires that began in
> earnest across a band from the Mediterranean to East
> Asia almost four thousand years ago. To the extent
> that we regard such international compacts as the
> European Union, GATT, and NAFTA as embodying
> imperial designs, furthermore, even today's requiem
> may prove premature.[13]

To this compact we must add the financialization of the globe.

Globalization plays with all the constituencies I have
announced in this chapter, but in a different way with the postcoloniality announced by the breakup of the old Russian imperial formation, competing with the Habsburgs and the
Ottomans, that managed to appropriate the dream of international socialism and was propelled by the historical moment

into new imperial competitions. In this sector of Comparative Literature, my example for the moment is Mark von Hagen's "From Russia to Soviet Union to Eurasia: A View from New York Ten Years After the End of the Soviet Union," a piece rich in suggestions for new work.[14]

The study of this new postcoloniality will not necessarily find the best directions from the proliferating collections of post-Soviet feminist anthologies in translation—first because, like much earlier postcolonial studies, they still follow the lines of empire, and therefore Central Asia is liable to find a less than interesting place, with little careful historical textualizing or tracing. And second, it is well known that the Soviets made women the vehicle of modernization in the area.[15] Thus here too the division among women on either side of the tradition-modernity line is one agenda for the new Comparative Literature as it weighs in with metropolitan Ethnic Studies. That particular division is quite often marked by access to Russian. The in-depth study of language is crucial here.

As Hamid Dabashi writes: "from the scattered memories of a sacred imagination that once congealed in the Arabia of the sixth (Christian) century, competing 'Islams' were invented by contending political forces dominant from Transoxiana to Spain."[16] The tribalities of Central Asia had paradoxically written a "freer," more eclectic Islam than the more publicized conflicts in the residue of medieval Islamic cosmopolitanism or the recent puritanism and orthodoxy of the Wahabis, and, in a different formation, the Taliban. Close as I am to Bangladesh, I am very aware of the paradoxical freedoms within peripheral Islams. In Central Asia we can tap the consequences of an earlier modernization of women and a current traditionalization of Islam. I have discussed the tracks of planetarity in this formation elsewhere.[17]

The range and diversity of the Islamic diaspora is immense. It is altogether appropriate that Comparative Literature should undo the politically monolithized view of Islam that rules the globe today, without compromising the strong unifying ideology potentially alive in that particular cultural formation.

Comparative Literature can also find its own unacknowledged prehistory in this sector, and thus do a long-range historical revision of the record of its apparently European provenance. Muslim Europe and Arabic–Persian cosmopolitanism have both been abundantly studied in Middle Eastern studies and comparative history.[18] Because of the special nature of Comparative Literature, we, on the other hand, have spent considerable energy on Leo Spitzer and Erich Auerbach in Turkey, as if they were explorers for the cause of literary criticism.[19]

To a certain extent, Islamic feminism has also been relegated to its own ghetto. The introduction to Deniz Kandiyoti's "Contemporary Feminist Scholarship and Middle East Studies" summarizes a great deal of information about this phenomenon.[20] I have attempted to work against such ghettoization in my work on Assia Djebar.[21]

Can the foothold for planetarity be located in the texts of these spread-out sectors of the world's literatures and cultures? Perhaps. The new comparativist is not obliged to look for them, of course. One cannot adjudicate the task of an entire discipline, in spite of the efforts of the world literaturists, the Encyclopedists. I think this drastic epistemic change must be imagined by Comparative Literature. But I cannot will everyone to think so.

I would like to close this section of the chapter with no more than a gesture toward the two older minorities, the

African American and the Hispanic. I am very far indeed from expertise in these areas. I have no doubt that intimations of planetarity in my sense have been documented in the vast critical literature in these areas. I give witness by quoting two passages from my own work, one on a passage from Toni Morrison, another on a passage from Diamela Eltit.[22] No plot summaries. As in the case of those teasers of the next mystery included at the end of thrillers, I hope the reader will move to the text if the bits tantalize. *Beloved* is a much-read text in the U.S. mainstream, Eltit not so.

First, then, a moment in *Beloved*:

The lesson of the impossibility of translation in the general sense, as Toni Morrison shows it, readily points at absolute contingency. Not the sequentiality of time, not even the cycle of seasons, but only weather, as in these words, summing up the conclusion of the terrible story of maternal sacrifice, an opening into a specifically African-American history. If Mahasweta undoes the division between Aboriginal and Indo-European India by the experience of an impossible planetarity; Morrison undoes the difference between Africa and African-America by the experience of a planetarity equally inaccessible to human time: "By and by, all traces gone. And what is forgotten is not only the footprints but the water and what it is down there. The rest is weather. Not the breath of the disremembered and unaccounted-for; but wind in the eaves, or spring ice thawing too quickly. Just weather" (*B*275).

That too is time. Geological time, however slow, is also time. One must not *make* history in a deliberate way. One must respect the earth's tone. One might be obliged to claim history from the violent perpetrator of it, in order to turn violation into the enablement of the individual, but that is another story. After the effacement of the trace, no project for restoring the origin. That is "just weather," here today as yesterday.

With this invocation of contingency, where nature may be the great body without organs of woman, we can begin to see that the project of translating culture within the politics of identity is not a quick fix.

And now "I give you the briefest glimpse of Diamela Eltit's *The Fourth World*, written during the so-called economic miracle following General Pinochet's repressive regime in Chile."[23]

Eltit achieves a sustained superrealism that signals another lexicon—an allegory to be explored—by its very seamlessness. The language mimes the tone of the child-analyst who knows that metaphor and reality—inner and outer—have not separated themselves in the child's consciousness. "Whole persons" have not congealed here. We are in a world of negotiable sexual identities, twin brother vanishing into twin sister. I repeat, nothing, except an uneasy sense of everything, tells us that there is an entire body of political meaning here—in order to discover which we must move into the social text. Far from being self-referential, the text signals beyond itself. Yet there will be no referential connection, I can promise. As soon as you decide this is a veiled description of a devastated country, you will be obliged to remind yourself what Melanie Klein teaches us: that this is the normal landscape of the infantile psyche that enters "social normality" precariously, in depression and mourning, which may or may not be informed with postcolonial content. Eltit does not permit negotiation between autobiography and the political: two discontinuous structures of violence.

The narrative, such as it is, begins with the primal scene of violence: "On that April 7, enshrouded in my mother's fever, I not only was conceived, but also must have shared her dream because I suffered the horrible feminine attack of dread" (FW3). After one hundred and eleven pages of violent shuttling and reality testing inching towards some unnameable conclusion, the last page asks for a reading in Kleinian language, as the birth of a political super-ego. When the beginning of the final section says "Outside . . . ," we are convinced that it is a description of a city on a certain map. There can be little doubt that "[t]he money from the sky return[ing] to the sky . . . hungry for urban emptiness but also sowing emptiness upon the fields . . . [upon which] contempt for the sudaca race [the immiserated female race, especially from the South—*sud*] is clearly printed" (FW112–113) speaks of the empty promise of "economic growth" as the immiseration not only of some place like Chile but of the entire South, of "Development"-as-exploitation. This is not post-colonial*ism* as some latter-day psychomachia of territorial imperialism. It is the recognition of a globality that cannot be captured by our computers. Autobiography is easy here—the collectors of testimonies are waiting with their tape recorders—but irrelevant. "Far away," the book concludes, "in a house abandoned to brotherhood, between April 7 and 8, diamela eltit, assisted by her twin brother, gives birth

to a baby girl. The sudaca baby will go up for sale"—
code name "democratization."

Today I would suggest that, by attempting to write the
self at its othermost and blurring the outlines between that
graphic and globalization, Eltit's text stages the lineaments of
the planetary.

[In response to objections from my first best reader, I had jet-
tisoned what I include in this extended parenthesis. Perhaps it
would have been wiser to excise. Let me at least give my rea-
sons for pasting the cut text back in.

All you're saying is that these two pluralize, my friend had
said. I cannot see how that can be read as planetarity.

What I am attempting is to force a reading. I would like to
see if the text could possibly sustain the turning of identitarian
monuments into documents for reconstellation. Twenty-five
years ago I attempted such a forced reading of *To the Lighthouse*, timidly attesting that it might not be "correct."[24] I still
recall a mainstream feminist critic mockingly commenting that
it was certainly an incorrect reading. I realize now that I have
not lost my obstinacy. I read in Miller's *Others*: "This other
calling on us to respond, this future that comes into being by
way of the response, can only get here, arrive on this shore,
speaking in tongues, in a multitude of overlapping and contradictory voices."[25] In Mark von Hagen's groundbreaking
"From Russia to Soviet Union to Eurasia," I read that a "consequence of this feature [the retelling of the history of the
Russian empire and Soviet Union from multiple vantage
points] of pluralization has been a decentering of Russian history"; that in the fourth issue of *Kritika*, a journal associated
with this new pluralization, "the editors defend their tolerance
of cultural studies approaches to 'representations of alterity.' "

I keep feeling that there are connections to be made that I cannot make, that pluralization may allow the imagining of a necessary yet impossible planetarity in ways that neither my reader nor I know yet. In this last chapter of scattered speculations, I include this imperfect parenthesis in the hope that the connection will be made by a future reader. As follows:

Identity politics is neither smart nor good. Comparative Literature laced with Area Studies goes rather toward the other. With this confidence, I approach two widely known, heroic figures from the older minorities, writers of a previous dispensation: José Martí (1853–1895) and W.E.B. Du Bois (1868–1963). The task is to find moments in these earlier texts that can be reinscribed for what I am calling planetarity.

José Martí, the Cuban activist intellectual who lived in New York from 1881 to 1895 and died in action in the Cuban revolution against Spanish colonialism, could still seem to generalize a binary opposition: "Spanish America, *his* America . . . [as] 'Our America' and . . . Anglo-Saxon America, 'the Other America.' "[26] If we look more closely at his writings, however, we see this fervent nationalist going beyond mere nationalism to a more general and heterogeneous version of "Latin America," a phrase coming into circulation even as he was writing.[27] I believe it is possible to read the concept-metaphors of Martí's ruralist left-humanism for undoing named binaries, nationalism giving way not only to a heterogeneous continentalism but also to an internationalism that can, today, shelter planetarity. I will read only one passage here, but examples can be multiplied. To read one passage is not to underdemonstrate the argument.

Forcing Martí onto the tracks of planetarity is particularly fraught with the temptation to "ruralism." I have written about the spectralization of the rural (altogether distinct from ruralism)—conversion of "the rural" into a database for pharmaceutical dumping, chemical fertilizers, patenting of indigenous knowledge, big dam building and the like—as the forgotten front of globalization for which the urban is an instrument.[28] In my open-plan fieldwork, I consider the Indian rural poor as the largest sector of the electorate. The urban subproletariat should certainly not be ignored. In order, however, to access cultural systems—long dysfunctional because of delegitimation—for the source of an ethical instruction that may supplement socialism, the isolation of the rural may be helpful. To romanticize this group as the primitive will defeat the purpose and annul effort. And indeed, I always insist that we should make a further effort, at the same time, to insert them into the social productivity of capital through education, a risky undertaking. But otherwise, the current material wretchedness of their normality is not perceived as due to the remote depredations of capitalist exploitation without capital's social productivity.[29]

It is from this position, far from a primitivist romanticization of the rural, that I ask, Is it possible to make Martí's ruralism into a *mochlos* for planetarity?[30] Since the Earth is a bigger concept-metaphor than bounded nations, located cities, can we read it against Martí's grain and turn the text around for planetarity? Perhaps not. As I have already indicated, I write for a future reader. In the meantime, let me not be taken to be a ruralist, quite in the grain of Martí's text.

My plane is flying now over the land between Baghdad, Beirut, Haifa, and Tripoli, into Turkey and Romania. I am making a clandestine entry into "Europe." Yet the land looks the same—hilly sand. I know the cartographic markers because of the TV in the arm of my seat. Planetarity cannot deny globalization. But, in search of a springboard for planetarity, I am looking not at Martí's invocation of the rural but at the figure of land that seems to undergird it. The view of the Earth from the window brings this home to me.

It is of course an established, even banal connection that exists between the rural and the Earth, Nature capital N. But even at its most banal it provides a countertext to the idea of city/nation. This is particularly noticeable when Martí speaks of education. Martí is no primitivist. His civic planning, however untested, inspired Fidel Castro as well as the Florida Cubans. His ideas of the education of the rural population are closer to Booker T. Washington than to Du Bois and more like the Chautauqua in form. But the logic of the metaphors rather than, necessarily, the substantive argument allows a way out of nationalism, and not in the direction of the North American diaspora. Nowhere is this clearer than in his account of the memorial service on the death of Karl Marx, where the idea of a labor international is embellished in the following way: "By operating the forces of Nature, they become as beautiful as Nature" (MR 43; translation modified).

It is when he is writing of the education of the peasant that the metaphor of nature releases its potential for displacement. In this account as well, he speaks of education. However bourgeois, sometimes even feudal, Martí's language might be, he intuits the same problem that Perry Anderson describes a hundred years later: the tension between structure and subject in Marx's thought. "Being in a hurry, and somewhat away from real life, he did not see that children who have not had a natural and laborious gestation are not born viable, whether in the womb of the people, in history, or from the womb of woman in the home" (MR 44; translation modified).[31] Again, the link is banal: nature, woman, and history by way of fertility. But the logic of the metaphor connects internationalism and nature, by placing history itself in the forces of nature and thus away from the specificity of nations. The common Spanish word for "people"—*el pueblo*—one of whose strong current meanings is "village," as one among a range of possible groupings of people, from a small local group to a tribe to a nation—manages the contrast between city/nation and nature.

Parallel structural contrasts—between nature and trade, universality and the nation—are present and managed in Martí's best-known piece on education, "Wandering Teachers" (MR 46–50). Here is the passage I will read: "The farmer's children cannot leave the paternal farm and day after day, go mile after mile, to learn Latin declensions and short division. And yet"—there is the contrast—

> The farmers comprise the best, most healthful, and succulent national mass, because they receive from up close and in full measure the emanations and the loving contact of the earth from whose loving give-and-take they live. Cities are the minds of nations; but their hearts, where the blood rushes back and from where it is redistributed, are in the countryside. Men are still eating machines. We must make every man a torch. (MR 48; translation modified)

The country here is not simply the prenational as opposed to the national. It is also the *hylè* or mass of the national, to which the blood rushes first and that becomes continuous with the exchange with the Earth. The Earth is a paranational image that can substitute for international and can perhaps provide, today, a displaced site for the imagination of planetarity. The choice of the blood rushing *back* as the first move, the description of the rural as a specifically *national* mass, and the inclusion of the trade-related word "redistribution" (*se repartir*) in its activity seeks to undo the contradiction between the national and the rural.[32] If you read these essays in the context of Martí's own development, the vision of the countryside as the place of national production and redistribution rather than consumption—leading to exchange—is clear. Martí's was a necessarily proleptic choice for a specifically *postcolonial* internationality. We will see this to be true of Du Bois's choice as well. In our conjuncture, I am asking if there is anything in these stirrings of a postcolonialism before the letter that can displace itself into planetarity. Can the figure of the rural in Martí gives us leverage for such a reading?

Martí was acutely aware of the internal line of *cultural* difference within "the same culture." He was against the establishment of a Creole oligarchy in postcolonial Cuba. This combines with left-ruralism in his work to reverse and displace the direction of progressive change, however imperfectly. This tendency can be developed to make his work consonant with the planetary imagination of the new Comparative Literature. We are outlining a politics of reading. Marx's preference for the city over the country could not think the spectralization of the rural yet.[33]

The question of the possible displacement into planetarity may be a necessary supplement to the reconfiguration of "Our America" for cultural studies, which suggests that "Martí's U.S. writing belongs to that tradition of exilic representation which counterpoises the lived experience of being 'left alone' in the Anglo United States with the reconstructed collective memories of homelands which lie elsewhere."[34] Martí is not quite so distant from Cuba when he writes from New York; he is constantly planning for his country's future. "Reconstructed collective memories" gives a sense of nostalgia that, for me, is absent from Martí's feisty text, except for some stylized poetry where the genre asks for that sentiment.[35] I think part of this sentimentalization is precisely because the text is being reconfigured for the "twentieth-century migration [that] has seen the reassertion of Our America's *cultural* claims to" the Other America. The essays in the collection from which I quote, especially those by Rosaura Sanchez and Donald Pease, redress the balance, pointing at the historical difference rather than effacing it by appropriation. I seek not only to correct but also to displace.

José Martí was killed fighting the Spanish at the age of forty-two. Du Bois was ninety-five when he died. We can see the possibility of being pulled into the track of planetarity more clearly in the latter. W. E. B. Du Bois undid African American continent-think, reversing and displacing the violence and violation of slavery and imperialism. In our historical moment, we must try persistently to reverse and displace globalization into planetarity—an impossible figure and therefore calling on *teleopoiesis* rather than *istoria*.

The Souls of Black Folk is the prototype of the best (nationalist) vision of metropolitan Cultural Studies.[36] Du Bois acknowledges the responsibility of the African *American* because "the shadow," as yet unpluralized, "of a mighty Negro past"—this metaphor of the shadow is important for him—must be claimed as part of an American past as well. The price is high. We can read a reversal of Aristotle's definition of friendship—one soul in two bodies—as we can read an echo of Faust's lament in Du Bois's description of the African American at the end of the last century as "two souls . . . in one dark body, whose dogged strength alone keeps it from being torn asunder" (SB 52).[37] Writing from the Indian subcontinent, Ashis Nandy had spoken of Britain as the intimate enemy.[38] For the African American, the intimate enemy resides inside. This difference animates what I discuss next, a prescient essay called "The Negro Mind Reaches Out," written twenty-five years later, where Du Bois gives us the first taste of colonial discourse studies and even a preview of what was to follow from it—postcolonial criticism. Du Bois the pan-Africanist knew the continent of Africa to be heterogeneous.

Du Bois's movement from exceptionalism to egalitarian-
ism—pushing for "the talented tenth" in the early phase to com-
munism in the later—is well known. If, however, we look at the
two texts without explicit reference to his intellectual life, what
seems most striking is that, writing as a member of the metropolitan minority, Du Bois is exceptionalist and individualist;
whereas, writing as a member of a global colonial world looking
forward to postcoloniality, Du Bois is altogether aware that the
production of the exceptionalist and individualist colonial subject creates a class division among the colonized, and that the
colonizer often and paradoxically preferred the "primitive"
rather than the "mimic man" he himself produced. Du Bois was
writing on the internal class line of which I spoke above. Today,
when these class divisions have altered the demographics of the
former colonies and their diasporas, the metropolitan comparativist must imagine planetarity, displace the "primitivism" of the
colonizer into the subaltern of the postcolonial, existing now in
a cultural formation historically compromised by centuries of
delegitimization; through the transforming work of imagining
the impossible other as that figured other imagines us.

In ripe colonialism, Du Bois writes of

the new democratic problems of colonization . . . fostered by a certain type of white colonial official who
was interested in the black man and wanted him to
develop. But this official was interested in the primitive
black and not in the educated black. He feared and
despised the educated West African and did not believe
him capable of leading his primitive brother. He sowed
seeds of dissension between these two. (NM 399)

Postcolonially, the relationship between "the educated West
African"—the Black European—and the "primitive" has con-

tinued in a class apartheid. The call for planetarity in the reading subject may be a training for at least recognizing that scandal in the history of the present.

Du Bois is aware of the results, first, of the difference among the imperial policies of the various European powers; and, second, of the difference in the imperial policy of the same power toward its various constituencies. Thus for Du Bois the production of the colonial subject is diversified, yet another lesson that some postcolonial work forgets explicitly, though its mark is historically evident upon its body, as academic interest broadens out into Development and human rights.

Let us consider these two points separately. As we do so, we must of course note that Du Bois presupposes the difference in the production of the New World African—historically a double ancestry claimed by struggle, and, in 1924, the date of "The Negro Mind Reaches Out," an economic and educational status more rooted, by that fact, as "American" than the Black European gentleman of whom he speaks.

Observing the difference in policy among the various European powers, or, as he puts it more picturesquely, the "shadows" of Portugal, Belgium, France, and England, Du Bois notices that "for nearly two centuries France has known educated and well-bred persons of Negro descent. . . . It was not that the French loved or hated Negroes as such; they simply grew to regard them as men with the possibilities and shortcomings of men, added to an unusual natural personal appearance" (NM 392). Alas, the situation is sadly changed today. And indeed, Du Bois did not see the shadow of France as an unquestioned good. Only in Boineuf of Martinique does he discover an exception: "One black deputy alone, Boineuf of Martinique, has the vision. His voice rings in Parliament. He made the American soldiers keep their hands off the Senegalese. He made the governor of Congo apologize and explain;

he made Poincaré issue that extraordinary warning against American prejudice. Is Boineuf an exception or a prophecy?" (NM 397). Frantz Fanon is born in Martinique the next year.

We cannot know if Du Bois was aware that anticolonialism would not lead to productive continentalism. If so, he never put it down in published writing. We can turn to Wole Soyinka, "Arms and the Arts," to find a clue, English to English, class-fixed.[39] The project for the new Comparative Literature would have been to make it possible to trace this multiform trajectory (or its restricted permeability) in the African languages, thickening each nation-state invoked by Soyinka through persistently depoliticized Area Studies resources. Insofar as such pluralization decenters the idea of "Africa," it is possible to think our way into considerations of subalternity, eminently present in African studies from Amadiume to Mudimbe (I am no expert), and perhaps take a step, learning to learn from below, toward imagining planetarity.[40]]

Just as socialism at its best would persistently and repeatedly wrench capital away from capitalism, so must the new Comparative Literature persistently and repeatedly undermine and undo the definitive tendency of the dominant to appropriate the emergent. It must not let itself be constituted by the demands of liberal multiculturalism alone. Training in such persistent and repetitive gestures comes, necessarily, in the classroom. Insofar as the tertiary student is in the service of the dominant (although often unwilling or unable to acknowledge it), such training might seem to undermine their self-assurance. This is not an easy "positional skepticism of postmodernist literary and cultural studies," but something to be worked through in the interest of yoking the humanities, however distantly, with however few guarantees, to a just world.[41] I appreciate gestures to shore up the humanities institutionally. I can, however, concur less with John Guillory's recent suggestion that "the appropriate alternative to this strategy is to define and develop a knowledge of culture fully integrated into the spectrum of human sciences" than I can with Moretti's scopic generic morphology (see chapter 2, note 1), which promises excellent reference tools, at least. Legitimating the humanities by making them scientific was already tried by the extremes of symbolic logic and structuralism, which were and are, in their own sphere, useful developments. Our own North American player Northrop Frye put in a strong bid for literary studies on the model of the "natural sciences," although he did grant that "the presence of incommunicable experience in the center of criticism will always keep criticism an art." This incommunicable experience had nothing to do with Frye's remarkably impersonal view of the ethical, as witness his "Second Essay: Ethical Criticism."[42] To confuse the ethical as the experience of the impossible with positional skepticism and prescribe scientific procedure, as does Guillory, speaks perhaps to the occupational hazard of wanting a science of criticism. If we want to compete with the hard "science"(s) and the social sciences at their hardest as "human science," we have already lost, as one loses institutional competition. In the arena of the humanities as the uncoercive rearrangement of desire, he who wins loses. If this sounds vague, what we learn (to imagine what we know) rather than know in the humanities remains vague, unverifiable, iterable. You don't put it aside in order to be literary critical.

The planetarity of which I have been speaking in these pages is perhaps best imagined from the precapitalist cultures of the planet. In this era of global capital triumphant, to keep responsibility alive in the reading and teaching of the textual is at first sight impractical. It is, however, the right of the textual to be so responsible, responsive, answerable. The "planet" is, here, as perhaps always, a catachresis for inscribing collective responsibility as right. Its alterity, determining experience, is mysterious and discontinuous—an experience of the impossible. It is such collectivities that must be opened up with the question "How many are we?" when cultural origin is detranscendentalized into fiction—the toughest task in the diaspora.

NOTES

1. CROSSING BORDERS

1. "Preface," in Charles Bernheimer, ed., *Comparative Literature in the Age of Multiculturalism* (Baltimore: Johns Hopkins University. Press, 1995), ix–x.

2. Toby Alice Volkman, *Crossing Borders: Revitalizing Area Studies* (New York: Ford Foundation, 1999), ix. This attempt—to rethink Area Studies after the Cold War—is now somewhat outdated. The watchword now is "Area Studies after 9/11," and the configuration resembles the earlier Area Studies initiative, which I discuss in my text. Here is an ex-

cerpt from a spring 2002 [Congressional] Conference Report for the Appropriations Act:

The conferees find that our national security, stability and economic vitality depend, in part, on American experts who have sophisticated language skills and cultural knowledge about the various areas of the world. An urgent need exists to enhance the nation's in-depth knowledge of world areas and transnational issues, and fluency of U.S. citizens in languages relevant to understanding societies where Islamic and/or Muslim culture, politics, religion, and economy are a significant factor.

Therefore, the conferees have included an increase of $20,478,000 for the Title VI/Fulbright-Hays programs to increase the number of international experts (including those entering government service and various professional disciplines) with in-depth expertise and high-level language proficiency in the targeted world areas of Central and South Asia, the Middle East, Russia, and the Independent States of the former Soviet Union. A portion of these funds is intended to enhance the capacity of U.S. higher education institutions to sustain these initiatives over time. The conferees encourage the creation of distance learning initiatives to provide more universal access to language training, summer language institutes abroad, one-on-one language tutoring to accelerate student progress to the highest levels of proficiency, engaging the language resources of local heritage communities where appropriate, and increased collaboration with the Title VI language resource centers, the centers for international business education and research, and the American overseas research centers with a focus on the least commonly taught languages and areas and underrepresented professional disciplines. (communication to Area Studies institutes holding Title VI grants)

At this point, to withdraw in-depth language learning and close reading from Comparative Literature when it moves to the global South is to decide that the only relationship the United States can have with those areas is based on considerations of security, that the critical intimacy of literary learning must remain isolationist in the Euro-U.S.

3. The statistics may have changed slightly in the intervening years, but the general picture remains the same.

4. George E. Rowe, "50th Anniversary of *Comparative Literature*" and Timothy Bahti, "Impossibility, Free," *Comparative Literature* 51 (1) (Winter 99): 1, 62. Bahti is right, *Premises* is a fine book, and the times are near Fascist, more so than in 1999. The solution is not to go back to an exclusivist Eurocentric comparative literature spawned in the late forties.

5. "Versions of the Margin: J. M. Coetzee's *Foe* Reading Defoe's *Crusoe/Roxana*,"in Jonathan Arac and Barbara Johnson, eds., *Consequences of Theory: Selected Papers of the English Institute, 1987–88* (Baltimore: Johns Hopkins University Press, 1990), 154; the lecture was delivered two years earlier.

6. Charles Wagley, *Area Research and Training: A Conference Report on the Study of World Areas* (New York: Columbia University, n.d.), 1; emphasis mine.

7. These sentiments are expressed in Margaret Talbot, "The Way We Live Now: 11-18-01; Other Woes" *New York Times Magazine*, November 18, 2001, 23, in the wake of September 11.

8. The groundbreaking energy of *Orientalism* by Edward W. Said (New York: Pantheon, 1978) tends to conflate Oriental Studies, Area Studies, and Comparative Literature. Enabled by its initiating impulse, we now make these distinctions.

9. The Birmingham metaphor is taken from the title of a book by one of the most brilliant students at the first Cultural Studies group: Paul Gilroy, *There Ain't No Black in the Union Jack: The Cultural Politics of Race and Nation* (New York: Routledge, 1992 [1987]). There are more differences than similarities here. These differences have been charted by Lawrence Grossberg in *Dancing in Spite of Myself: Essays on Popular Culture* (Durham: Duke University Press, 1997), 191–218.

10. For "ontopologist," see Jacques Derrida, *Specters of Marx: the State of the Debt, the Work of Mourning, and the New International*, tr. Peggy Kamuf (New York: Routledge, 1994), 82. In a back issue of *The New Yorker* (June 23 & 30, 1997), Salman Rushdie refers to all the literatures of India not in English as "parochial."

11. Gayatri Chakravorty Spivak, "Translation as Culture," *parallax* 6 (1) (Jan.-Mar. 2000): 21.

12. When I make this point, I often hear "But everyone can't learn all the languages!" Just as the old Comparative Literature did not require learning "all the European languages," so also does this new version of Comparative Literature not ask you to learn all the world's languages. The only requirement is that, when you work with literatures of the global South, you learn the pertinent languages with the same degree of care. As you go toward the already available resources of Area Studies, learn the language with literary depth rather than only social scientific fluency.

13. Jacques Derrida, *Given Time: I. Counterfeit Money*, tr. Peggy Kamuf (Chicago: University of Chicago Press, 1992), 54; the next reference is to 67.

14. "Righting Wrongs." In Nicholas Owen, ed., *Human Rights and Human Wrongs* (Oxford: Oxford University Press, 2003).

15. As usual, Raymond Williams's system of residual-dominant-emergent-archaic-preemergent gives me the best handle on mapping culture as process (Raymond Williams, *Marxism and Literature* [Oxford: Oxford University Press, 1977], 121–127). This is why I began with an account of academic memos, a mundane record of the dominant appropriating a social emergent.

16. 1999 Report of the Mayor's Task Force on CUNY, chaired by Benno C. Schmidt Jr., entitled, "The City University of New York: An Institution Adrift." The passage quoted is from 13.

17. Mehdi Charef, *Le Thé Au Harem d'Archi Ahmed* (Paris: Mercure de France, 1983). The phrase is an Arabic transformation of the theorem of Archimedes worked out by a young North African immigrant boy in the low-income housing projects in the outskirts of Paris. This is a typical example of how the underclass imagination swims in the deep waters of metropolitan survival.

18. Derrida, "Force of Law," in *Acts of Religion*, tr. Gil Anidjar (New York: Routledge, 2002), 249: translation modified.

19. What follows is my own interpretative digest of Melanie Klein, *Works* (New York: Free Press, 1984), vols. 1–4. Giving specific footnotes is therefore impossible. The details may also not resemble orthodox Kleinian psychoanalysis.

20. Spivak, "Translation as Culture," 13.

21. For the definition of irony I am using here, see Paul de Man, *Allegories of Reading: Figural Language in Rousseau, Nietzsche, Rilke and Proust* (New Haven: Yale University Press, 1979), 301.

22. Jacques Derrida, *The Monolingualism of the Other*, tr. Patrick Mensah (Stanford: Stanford University Press, 1998), 57–58.

23. Maryse Condé, *Heremakhonon* (Boulder: Three Continents, 1985), 24.

24. Maryse Condé, *En attendant le bonheur (Heremakhonon)* (Paris: Seghers, 1988), 12.

25. Derrida has an uncharacteristically hardheaded comment about the poor souls who must cross to Europe to seek refuge or escape from poverty: "Today, on this earth of humans, certain people must yield to the homo-hegemony of dominant languages. They must learn the language of the masters, of capital and machines; they must lose their idiom in order to survive or live better" (Derrida, *Monolingualism*, 30).

26. Michael Gomez, *Pragmatism in the Age of Jihad: The Precolonial State of Bundu* (Cambridge: Cambridge University Press, 1992), 22–23.

27. Saskia Sassen, discussion after Keynote, Conference on Comparative Literature in Transnational Times, Princeton University, March 23–24, 2000.

28. Volkman, *Crossing Borders*, ix.

29. J. M. Coetzee, *Waiting for the Barbarians* (New York: Penguin, 1982), 51.

30. Mary Louise Pratt, "Comparative Literature and Global Citizenship," in Bernheimer, ed., *Comparative Literature in the Age of Multiculturalism* (Baltimore: Johns Hopkins University. Press, 1995), 58.

31. Coetzee, *Waiting*, 30; the next quoted passage is from 81.

32. Sigmund Freud, "The Uncanny," in *The Standard Edition of the Psychological Works*, tr. Alix Strachey et al. (New York: Norton, 1961–), 17:221, hereafter cited in the text as UC, with page numbers following.

2. COLLECTIVITIES

1. A word about Franco Moretti's brilliant and witty essay about training for new global encyclopedias, although it claims to describe the entire burden of a global comparative literature (Moretti, "Conjectures on World Literature," *New Left Review* n.s. 1 [Jan.–Feb. 2000]: 54–68). Such training relates to both assuming the subjectship of humanism and controlling undecidability. As he admits, it depends on the close reading practiced by national literary scholars on the periphery. Should our only

ambition be to create authoritative totalizing patterns depending on untested statements by small groups of people treated as native informants? There is something disingenuous about using Goethe, Marx, and Weber as justification for choosing world systems theory to establish a law of evolution in literature, especially since Marx and Engels were celebrating the in-itself-dubious achievements of the bourgeoisie and the world market. Imperialism is supposed to have brought the novel everywhere. Is the novel form identical with "literature"? I think the real problem with this identification, between writing good reference tools for the novel form on the one hand and for the entire discipline on the other, is a denial of collectivity. The others provide information while we know the whole world. Why should the (novel in the) whole world as our object of investigation be the task of every comparativist, who should give up on language learning? Is it not trivially true that the word "comparative" in "comparative literature" is more a distinguishing mark than a signifier? How can "close reading" be the hallmark of the United States "(in all its incarnations, from the new criticism to deconstruction)" (57), when the new Moretti-style comparativist must rely on close reading from the periphery? Should one point out that now may be the exactly wrong moment to follow the youngish Marx at his most totalizing? Here are Tom Nairn's words about Marx and "world literature": "the world market, world industries and world literature predicted with such exultation in *The Communist Manifesto* all conducted, in fact, to the world of nationalism" (Nairn, *The Break-up of Britain* [London: Verso, 1981], 341). And indeed, this *is* nationalism, U.S. nationalism masquerading as globalism. Manifest destiny carried the United States hallmark before close reading did.

The world systems theorists upon whom Moretti relies are now producing sinocentric systems that are equally useless for literary study—that must depend on texture—because they equate economic with cultural systems. In fact, most close reading comparativists do not only read a few texts. They spread out and rely on good reference instruments such as Moretti will provide. They consult secondary texts based on other peoples' close readings, as Moretti will. Where they *can* closely read, they see the "criticism" provided by the encyclopedist as necessarily superficial and unsatisfactory. The real problem is the claim to scopic vision: "I will dwell, as on some delicious game, on this method that makes anything appear at will in a particular stretching. . . . I will go so far as to say that this fascination complements what geometral researches into perspective allow to escape from vision. How is it that nobody has ever thought of connecting this with . . . the effect of an erection? Imagine a tattoo traced on the sexual organ *ad hoc* in the state of its repose and assuming its, if I may say so, developed form in another state" (Jacques Lacan, "Of the Gaze as *Objet petit a*," in *The Four Fundamental Concepts of Psycho-Analysis*, tr. Alan Sheridan [London: Hogarth Press, 1977], 87–88). For a more extended consideration of Moretti's essay, see Jonathan Arac, "Anglo-Globalism?" *New Left Review* 16 (July/Aug.); 35–45.

2. Jacques Derrida, *Politics of Friendship*, tr. George Collins (New York: Verso, 1997). Hereafter cited in text as PF, with page reference following.

3. Stuart Hall, "The Multicultural Question," in Barnor Hesse, ed., *Un/settled Multiculturalisms: Diasporas, Entanglements, "Transruptions"* (London: Zed Books, 2000), 209–241. On the other side, see Richard Rorty, *Contingency, Irony, and Solidarity* (Cambridge: Cambridge University Press, 1989) and Robert D. Kaplan, *Warrior Politics: Why Leadership Demands a Pagan Ethos* (New York: Random House, 2002).

4. This is an important moment in Husserl for Derrida. In *Adieu*, for example, it is precisely through this that he connects Husserlian phenomenology and Levinasian ethics: "a *certain* interruption of phenomenology by itself already imposed itself upon Husserl, though he did not, it is true, take note of it as an ethical necessity. . . . This became necessary in the *Cartesian Meditations* precisely when it was a question of the other; of an *alter ego* that never makes itself accessible except by way of an appresentational analogy and so remains radically separated, inaccessible to originary perception. . . . Levinas himself considers this interruption of self to be a 'paradox' . . . [that] 'requires a description that can be formed only in ethical language" (Derrida, *Adieu to Emmanuel Levinas*, tr. Pascale-Anne Brault and Michael Naas [Stanford: Stanford University Press, 1999], 51–53). We are in the arena, therefore, not of the stoppage of politics but of the relationship between ethics and politics that is crucial to Derrida's work.

5. We are not speaking of "good" politics here, but a politics that wrenches itself away from the certainties of the self. Such projective teleopoiesis requires the inclusion of "evil laughter." I am not about to literalize this into a predictive future. I would simply like to suggest that this phrase, in which both words are important, may indicate how far we

go from our high serious certainties when we undertake the imaginative task of moving out of ourselves.

6. Virginia Woolf, *A Room of One's Own* (New York: Harper, 1989), 84. Hereafter cited in text as RO, with page reference following.

7. Rosalind Morris is helping me wade through the large body of critical writing on this, although it does not touch the question of subaltern cultural formations.

8. It is at least as old as Friedrich Engels, *Origin of the Family, Private Property, and the State* (New York: International Publishers, 1972), first published in 1884.

9. Gayatri Chakravorty Spivak, *Imperatives to Re-Imagine the Planet/Imperative zur Neuerfindung des Planeten*, ed. Willi Goetschel (Vienna: Passagen, 1999).

10. Walter Benjamin, "Critique of Violence," in *Reflections: Essays, Aphorisms, Autobiographical Writing*, tr. Edmund Jephcott (New York: Schocken, 1978), 297.

11. J. M. Coetzee, *Disgrace* (New York: Penguin, 1999).

12. Benjamin Conisbee Baer has an excellent analysis of the Saatchi brothers' role in the art world, with examples like "the defenses of artistic expression manifested at the Brooklyn Museum in response to Giuliani's censorious threats . . . to 'Sensation: Young British Artists from the Saatchi Collection,' " and "funding student places at art schools," all of which he calls "the dominant *producing* the emergent" (private communication).

13. "Righting Wrongs," in Nicholas Owens, ed., *Human Rights and Human Wrongs* (Oxford: Oxford University Press, 2002).

14. Gayatri Chakravorty Spivak, *Thinking Academic Freedom in Gendered Post-Coloniality* (Cape Town: University of Cape Town Press, 1993); excerpt in Joan Vincent, ed., *The Anthropology of Politics* (Oxford: Blackwell, 2002).

15. In his lecture series "The Politics of the Governed," Partha Chatterjee has suggested that the part of the *postcolonial* polity that was kept out of the colonial subject production in colonialism proper has now found a political style that bypasses Enlightenment expectations of a civil society. His examples are fascinating, but I think, first, that they will not qualify as disrupting a *global* polity; and, second, that the lineaments of an ab-use of the Enlightenment (see his note 12) are already present there (Partha Chatterjee, "The Politics of the Governed," Leonard Hastings Schoff Memorial Lectures, Columbia University, November 2001).

16. I prefer this translation of *Médecins sans frontières* rather than the usual "doctors without borders" because their humanitarian mission makes it juridicopolitically easier for them to cross frontiers from above than for their beneficiaries to cross from below. I have no moral position on this. I merely wish not to celebrate the juridicopolitical transformation (translation?) of frontiers into borders in the English translation.

17. Roman Jakobson, "Concluding Statement," in Thomas Sebeok, ed., *Style in Language* (Cambridge: MIT Press, 1960), 370.

18. By "transnational" I mean "U.S."—ironically—as do the authors of "Constructing Global Feminism"—without irony (Valerie Sperling, et al., "Constructing Global Feminism: Transnational Advocacy Networks," *Signs* 26 [4] [Summer '01]: 1155–1186).

19. Gertrude Stein, "The Mother of Us All" (1946) in *Last Operas and Plays* (Baltimore: Johns Hopkins University Press, 1995), 80–81.

20. *The Stream of Life*, tr. Elizabeth Lowe and Earl Fitz (Minneapolis: University of Minnesota Press, 1989), 3. Cited in Hélène Cixous, "Contes de la différence sexuelle," in Mara Negrón and Anne Berger, eds., *Lectures de la différence sexuelle* (Paris: des femmes, 1994), 62, where she herself speaks of the fear of beginning.

21. Percy Bysshe Shelley, "A Defence of Poetry," in *Shelley's Critical Prose* (Lincoln: University of Nebraska Press, 1967), 29.

22. Luce Irigaray, *Democracy Begins Between Two* (London: Athlone Press, 2000).

23. Jacques Derrida, *The Other Heading: Reflections on Today's Europe*, tr. Pascale-Anne Brault and Michael B. Naas (Bloomington: Indiana University Press, 1992); Étienne Balibar, "Ambiguous Universality," *Differences* 7 (I) (Spring '95): 54, 61.

24. Joan C. Tronto, *Moral Boundaries: A Political Argument for an Ethic of Care* (New York: Routledge, 1993), x. The next passage is from 2–3.

25. Sumit Sarkar, *Modern India: 1885–1947* (Delhi: Macmillan, 1983), 310–311.

26. Jon Elster, *Ulysses and the Sirens: Studies in Rationality and Irrationality* (Cambridge: Cambridge University Press, 1979), 111.

27. Joseph Conrad, *Heart of Darkness and the Secret Sharer* (New York: Bantam, 1969), 9.

28. This is no more a cliché ("Kurtz's degradation is an example of the familiar narrative cliché of the European who 'goes native'," J. Hillis Miller, "Joseph Conrad: Should We Read *Heart of Darkness*?," in *Others*

[Princeton: Princeton University Press, 2001], 129) than it is a cliché to "justify" the novel as literature by claiming that it is "literature in the modern Western sense" (114, 115): " 'Literature' as we Westerners know it is a radically overdetermined historical product belonging only to Western societies" (113).

29. I am grateful to Robert Folkenflick for this insight.

30. "Out there. . . . On the edge of the world, in flaming deserts, mangled jungles, squelchy swamps, missionaries save the needy. Out there, the darkness. But for me, for Du, In Here, safety. At least, for now. Oh, the wonder, the wonder" (Bharati Mukherjee, *Jasmine* [New York: Grove Weidenfeld, 1989], 21).

31. Tayeb Salih, *Season of Migration to the North*, tr. Denys Johnston-Davies (Portsmouth, NH: Heinemann, 1970); hereafter cited in text as SM, followed by page reference. Mahasweta Devi, "Pterodactyl, Puran Sahay, and Pirtha," in *Imaginary Maps*, tr. Gayatri Chakravorty Spivak (New York: Routledge, 1995), 95–196; hereafter cited in text as IM, followed by page reference. Jennifer Wenzel's " 'The Same Book Many Times': Nostalgia, Africa, and Some Versions of the Third World" (paper presented at panel on "Who Needs the Third World?," annual convention, Modern Language Association, 2001) makes this important comment: "Undoing the coevalness of Europe and the Congo erases the material links between the two places—Congo rubber in Dunlop tires, Congo coltan in the cellphone in your pocket—and transforms the Congo into a primitivist psychological playground, an ahistorical state of mind, a measure of the First World's distance from its own pre-history." Another kind of connection that must be foreclosed.

32. Chinua Achebe, "An Image of Africa: Racism in Conrad's *Heart of Darkness*," in *Hopes and Impediments* (New York: Doubleday, 1988), 4.

33. Henry Staten, the first reader of this book in its manuscript form, suggests a reading of *Heart of Darkness* structured around the interruptions of Marlow's narrative. This could be another indication of the intertextuality of that text with this. In *Heart of Darkness*, in Staten's reading, the structure of interruption expresses the tensions in the question of collectivity that arise between Marlow and his companions on the boat around the issue of the bad loner whom he narrates. Although, as Staten knows, this reading engages only the Europeans, when cobbled to my reading of Salih, it can create an interesting exchange.

34. "Surmounted time." I am reading this as a figuration of Levinas's notion that "memory," "thought . . . anterior to the world to which it is posterior . . . is precisely the achievement of this ontological structure . . . [of] a home . . . the feat of having limited a part of this world and having closed it off" (Emmanuel Levinas, *Totality and Infinity: An Essay on Exteriority*, tr. Alphonso Lingis [Pittsburgh: Duquesne University Press, 1969], 169–170). Such a thought displaces the distinction between tradition and modernity by inscribing both in the phenomenology of the subject.

35. I am grateful to Joseph Massad for guiding me through the Arabic text.

36. The best nontechnical account of such a way of reading is still Roland Barthes, "Introduction to the Structural Analysis of Narratives," in *Image/Music/Text*, tr. Stephen Heath (New York: Noonday Press, 1988), 79–124.

37. Salih is a male author commendably grappling with the problem of tradition and modernity through the figuration of gender. In the last pages of "Moving Devi" (in Gayatri Chakravorty Spivak, *Other Asias* [Oxford: Blackwell, forthcoming]) I have indicated a failure of a comparable understanding of collectivity in Pankaj Butalia's *Moksha*.

38. For a-chrony, see Mieke Bal, *Narratology: Introduction to the Theory of Narrative* (Toronto: University of Toronto Press, 1997), 66–68.

39. *Ihar cheye hotem jodi arab-bedouin/payer toley bishal moru digontey hileen* . . . (If only I'd been Arab-Bedouin rather than what I am/With the great horizon-kissing desert under my feet . . .), a line from a famous poem by Rabindranath Tagore learned as a child, long before I had any informed idea about Bedouin culture, already established them in the formative imagination of a Bengali child as the epitome of a free life. For a similar yet different appropriation of the idea of the nomad for theory, see El-Mokhtar Ghambou, "Nomadism and Its Frontiers" (Ph.D. diss., New York University, 2000).

40. For a provocative treatment of cultural imperatives, see Greg Urban, *Metaculture: How Culture Moves Through the World* (Minneapolis: University of Minnesota Press, 2001), 145. A reading imperative such as this assumes cultural change, forever around the corner.

41. *Social Text* 15 (Fall '86): 65–88.

42. For other uses of this imperialist topos, see my discussion of Kipling, glossed by the historical account in David Arnold's work, in Spi-

vak, *Critique of Postcolonial Reason: Toward a History of the Vanishing Present* (Cambridge: Harvard University Press, 1999), 157–160.

3. PLANETARITY

1. In Wai Chee Dimock's excellent piece, "Literature for the Planet" (*PMLA* 116 [1] [Jan. '01]: 173–188), for example, the argument is that a classic of European literature may become timeless because people all over the world may feel moved by it at other times. The "Muslim" who seems to indicate planetarity is the great Muslim *European* Averröes. The contrast is between Osip Mandelstam's eclectic Dante and T. S. Eliot's Latin Dante. This good argument for the ahistoricity of literature, which echoes Shelley's powerful argument in *A Defence of Poetry*, is not the effortful epistemic shift I am imagining. Dimock's erudite essay remains confined to Euro–U.S. debates. The effort to learn the detail of other histories (the Gandhi–Irwin Pact for *A Room of One's Own*) is dismissed as "an almost automatic equation between the literary and the territorial," this identified with the "premise [of] the influential work of Benedict Anderson" (175). I am hoping for a collaboration with the social sciences (represented here by Anderson, say), so that both Comparative Literature and Area Studies can be transformed and prosper. Undergirding this joint venture is my prayer for planetary. Insofar as she claims *poiesis* over *istoria*, I am in complete solidarity with Dimock.

2. Gayatri Chakravorty Spivak, "Subaltern Studies: Deconstructing Historiography," in Donna Landry and Gerald MacLean, eds., *The Spivak Reader* (New York: Routledge, 1996), 226.

3. Luce Irigaray, "Plato's *Hystera*," in *Speculum of the Other Woman*, tr. Gillian C. Gill (Ithaca: Cornell University Press, 1985), 243–364.

4. Sandra M. Gilbert and Susan Gubar, *The Madwoman in the Attic: The Woman Writer and the Nineteenth-Century Literary Imagination* (New Haven: Yale University Press, 1979).

5. For the mismatch between morphology and narrative, see Jacqueline Rose, "Dora—Fragment of an Analysis," in *Sexuality in the Field of Vision* (London: Verso, 1986), 27–47.

6. Frederick Crews, "Conrad's Uneasiness—and Ours," in *Out of My System: Psychoanalysis, Ideology, and Critical Method* (New York: Oxford University Press, 1975), 42–62, offers a psychoanalytic reading of *Heart of*

Darkness that relates to Conrad's life and literary motives. He quotes Dr. Bernard C. Meyer, who reads Conrad's heroes as "postponing their long-awaited return to a mother" (47). It is not clear to me that he is using specifically Freudian vocabulary when he calls "Marlow's adventure" "an uncanny self-unfolding" (55). I am not qualified to read the textuality of Conrad's life. And I am not suggesting that the book is a representation of the unconscious, assuming that there is an unconscious to be represented. I am suggesting that Conrad may share the permissible narratives of European gentlemen at the turn of the nineteenth century, and that Freud's assigning of a definitive content to the uncanny is historical. Another permissible narrative offers the book its aporia: to render justice or fail to do so through a lie that is necessary to protect a woman, Kurtz's Intended.

7. In his otherwise brilliant and well-documented essay on *Heart of Darkness*, J. Hillis Miller misrepresents Achebe's essay by only "quoting" one passage from it twice ("Conrad was a bloody racist"), with no footnote reference to this complex and powerful piece. He also strongly implies that Achebe is incapable of reading the book "as literature, as opposed to [taking it] as a straightforwardly mimetic or referential work that would allow the reader to hold Conrad himself directly responsible for what is said as though he were a journalist or a travel writer" (Miller, "Joseph Conrad: Should We Read *Heart of Darkness*?," in *Others* [Princeton: Princeton University Press, 2001], 108, 111, 123). By reading Schlegel, Dickens, Eliot, Trollope, Conrad, Yeats, Forster, Proust, Derrida, and de Man in the name "of a radical otherness mediated in multiple ways by literary works" (2), Miller almost justifies Moretti's claim that the close readers read a small canon. It is not my position that the radically other can be mediated; but my position—that the radically other is impossibly figured, perhaps—I have developed repeatedly in my text. The point here is that, in spite of the carapace of multiple ironies, the passages I quote "mean," as the passages indicating irony "mean" for Miller. And Achebe's question is precisely that: Can we call a "classic" a work that requires such "meanings" of Africa in order for its ironies to operate? That question may be answered in many ways, each entailing a politics. But Achebe should not be dismissed without reference as an incompetent reader of a " 'literature [that] as we Westerners know it is a radically overdetermined product belonging only to Western societies" (113; I have quoted this sentence in the previous chapter as well)! That is part of the problem in Conrad's text that we are discussing. In order to make its fictive case about an indeterminate position

about imperialism, Africa must nonetheless be figured as inhuman, scary because it may not be.

8. Donald E. Pease, "US Imperialism: Global Dominance Without Colonies," in Sangeeta Ray and Henry Schwarz, eds., *A Companion to Postcolonial Studies* (Oxford: Blackwell, 2000), 203–220.

9. Joan Scott, "Experience," in Judith Butler and Joan Scott, eds., *Feminists Theorize the Political* (New York: Routledge, 1992), 22–40.

10. Gayatri Chakravorty Spivak, "Teaching for the Times," in *Red Thread* (Cambridge: Harvard University Press, forthcoming). As the Lexicon tells us, the second word is a much better derivation. What I was pointing at is that in contemporary metropolitan identitarianism, the distinction had collapsed. In this book, I have gone on to suggest that liberal multiculturalism, as uneasily espoused by the Bernheimer collection, allows the ethics of alterity to be overwritten as a politics of identity. I should mention that my knowledge of Arabic, classical Greek, and Spanish is minimal. I hope my attempt at "reading" them will show that we need not wait for expertise to question translation as the final solution or to valorize distant reading. For Arabic, I read painstakingly with a superb reader, not just a native speaker. For Spanish and classical Greek, I made the first attempt; my first reader corrected me. Such support must be sought in the academic community.

11. Jacques Derrida, *Monolingualism of the Other; or, The Prosthesis of Origin*, tr. Patrick Mensah (Stanford: Stanford University Press, 1998), 14.

12. Wu Hung, "Public Time, Public Portrait, and the Renewal of Urban Monumentality," "Photography and the Birth of a Modern Visual Culture of Fragments," and "Reinventing Exhibition Spaces in Post-Cultural Revolution China," conference on "Public Criticism and Visual Culture," Hong Kong University, June 6–10, 2002. Leo Ou-fan Lee and Liuo Ping-hueh presented brilliant discussions of spectacular nineteenth- and early twentieth-century verbal and visual texts focused toward correcting views expressed in Benedict Anderson's latest book, *The Spectre of Comparisons: Nationalism, South East Asia, and the World* (New York: Verso, 1998). The new Comparative Literature would find comparable efforts in other colonized countries, in India (there are parallels), and in North and sub-Saharan Africa, and make visible patterns in colonial production by the colonized middle class that would, incidentally, correct Anderson.

13. Charles Tilly, "How Empires End," in Karen Barkey and Mark von Hagen, eds., *After Empire: Multiethnic Societies and Nation-Building;*

The Soviet Union and the Russian, Ottoman, and Habsburg Empires (New York: Westview, 1997), 2.

14. Paper presented at conference on "Ten Years of Post-Soviet Historiography," Ost und Sudosteuropa-Institut, University of Vienna, September 2001, and under consideration at *American History Review*.

15. Gregory Massell, *The Surrogate Proletariat: Moslem Women and Revolutionary Strategies in Soviet Central Asia, 1919–1929* (Princeton: Princeton University Press, 1974).

16. Hamid Dabashi, *Truth and Narrative: The Untimely Thoughts of 'Ayn Al-Qudat Al-Hamadhani* (Richmond, Surrey: Curzon Press, 1999), 109.

17. With the opening of the Oil Road, we will see a quick restructuring of Central Asian economies to accommodate aggressive financialization. Women's microcredit initiatives without infrastructural involvement become a part of this. For my discussion of planetarity in tribal Islam, see *Imperatives to Re-Imagine the Planets/Imperative zur Neuerfindung des Planeten*, ed. Willi Goetschel (Vienna: Passagen, 1999).

18. For Muslim Europe, Reinhart Dozy, *Spanish Islam*, tr. Francis Griffin Stokes (London: Chatto and Windus, 1913); H. A. R. Gibb, *The Influence of Islamic Culture on Medieval Europe* (Manchester: John Rylands Library, 1955); and Jean Lacam, *Les Sarrazins dans le haut moyen-age français* (Paris: Maisonneuve, 1965) represent the tip of the iceberg, indicating the monumental, the secondary, and the orientalist tendencies. For Islamic cosmopolitanism, see George Makdisi, *The Rise of Colleges: Institutions of Learning in Islam and the West* (Edinburgh: Edinburgh University Press, 1981), and *The Rise of Humanism in Classical Islam and the Christian West with Special Reference to Scholasticism* (Edinburgh: Edinburgh Univresity Press, 1990). I thank Hamid Dabashi for his help in compiling this brief checklist.

19. I hasten to add that these are excellent provocative essays. I am suggesting that they be supplemented by other histories. For the moment, the important examples may be Emily Apter, "Comparative Exile: Competing Margins in the History of Comparative Literature," in the Bernheimer volume, 86–96; and Aamir R. Mufti, "Auerbach in Istanbul: Edward Said, Secular Criticism and the Question of Minority Culture," in Paul A. Bové, ed., *Edward Said and the Work of the Critic: Speaking Truth to Power* (Durham: Duke University Press, 2000), 229–256.

20. In Deniz Kandiyoti, ed., *Gendering the Middle East: Emerging Perspectives* (Syracuse, NY: Syracuse University Press, 1996), 1–27.

21. Gayatri Chakravorty Spivak, "Acting Bits/Identity Talk," *Critical Inquiry* 18 (4) (Summer 1992): 770–773; "Ghost-Writing," *Diacritics* 25 (2) (Summer 1995): 78–82.

22. Spivak, "Acting Bits," 793–794; "Three Women's Texts and Circumfession," in Alfred Hornung and Ernstpeter Ruhe, eds., *Postcolonialism and Autobiography* (Amsterdam: Rodopi, 1998), 21–22.

23. Diamela Eltit, *The Fourth World*, tr. Dick Gerdes (Lincoln: University of Nebraska Press, 1995). Hereafter cited in text as FW, with page reference following.

24. Gayatri Chakravorty Spivak, "Unmaking and Making in *To the Lighthouse*," subsequently included in a revised version in *In Other Worlds: Essays in Cultural Politics* (New York: Methuen, 1987), 30–45.

25. Miller, *Others*, 273–274.

26. Philip Foner, "Introduction" in José Martí, *Our America* (New York: Monthly Review Press, 1977), 24.

27. The OED's first index entry for Latin America is from 1890, the U.S. State Department's "Reciprocity Treaties with Latin America," but such a term enters official use when it has been around for a little while, of course. For its itinerary, see Angel G. Loureiro, "Spanish Nationalism and the Ghost of Empire," forthcoming in the *Journal of Spanish Cultural Studies*.

28. Gayatri Chakravorty Spivak, "Love, Cruelty, and Cultural Talks in the Hot Peace," in Pheng Cheah and Bruce Robbins, eds., *Cosmopolitics: Thinking and Feeling Beyond the Nation* (Minneapolis: University of Minnesota Press, 1998), 329–348.

29. Marx had spoken of this combination in connection with foreign trade in *Capital*, tr. David Fernbach (New York: Vintage, 1981), 3: 344–347.

30. For *mochlos*, see Jacques Derrida, "Mochlos; or, The Conflict of the Faculties," in *Logomachia: The Conflict of the Faculties* (Lincoln: University of Nebraska Press, 1992), 1–34.

31. Perry Anderson, *In the Tracks of Historical Materialism* (New York: Verso, 1983).

32. I am told that the "*re*" in "*repartir*" does not necessarily have the same force as the "re" in "redistribution." This does not interfere with the idea that the blood rushes *back* to the heart and is then shared out— a figure of exchange.

33. I have discussed this in Spivak, "From Haverstock Hill Flat to U.S. Classroom, What's Left of Theory?" in Judith Butler et al., eds. *What's Left of Theory?: New Work on the Politics of Literary Theory* (New York: Routledge, 2000), 1–40.

34. Jeffrey Belnap and Raúl Fernández, "Introduction," in *José Martí's "Our America"* (Durham, NC: Duke University Press, 1998), 6.

35. One such poem is discussed by Julio Ramos in "Migratories," in Julio Rodríguez-Luis, ed., *Re-reading José Martí: One Hundred Years Later* (Albany: SUNY Press, 1999), 53–58.

36. W. E. B. Du Bois, *The Souls of Black Folk* (New York: Signet, 1995 [1903]); hereafter cited in text as SB, with page references following.

37. Johann Wolfgang von Goethe, *Faust*, tr. Walter Kaufmann (Garden City, NY: Doubleday, 1963), 145. Cornel West has tracked this passage to Emerson in *The American Evasion of Philosophy: A Genealogy of Pragmatism* (Madison: University of Wisconsin Press, 1989), 144.

38. Ashis Nandy, *The Intimate Enemy: Loss and Recovery of Self Under Colonialism* (Delhi: Oxford University Press, 1983).

39. Wole Soyinka, *Arms and the Arts: A Continent's Unequal Dialogue* (Cape Town: University of Cape Town, 1999).

40. Ifi Amadiume, *Male Daughters, Female Husbands: Gender and Sex in African Society* (London: Zed Books, 1987); V. Y. Mudimbe, *The Idea of Africa* (Bloomington: Indiana University Press, 1994). If in the case of Martí we had to circumvent the metaphor of woman-mother-earth proactively, concatenating Du Bois with feminism is a more labor-intensive task. The Black European is not only class-fixed but gender-fixed as well. For deep background articulated, see Brent Hayes Edwards, "One More Time," *Transition* 89 (2001): 88–107, a review of David Levering Lewis, *W.E.B. Du Bois: The Fight for Equality and the American Century, 1919–1963* (New York: Henry Holt, 2000), which discusses Du Bois's sexuality in some detail.

41. John Guillory, "The Sokal Affair and the History of Criticism," *Critical Inquiry* 28 (2) (Winter 2002): 501. The next passage is from the same paragraph.

42. Northrop Frye, *Anatomy of Criticism* (New York: Atheneum, 1968), 27–28, 71–128.

INDEX